PERSONAL LIABILITY OF MANAGERS AND SUPERVISORS FOR CORPORATE EEO POLICIES AND DECISIONS

By

Daniel R. Levinson

EQUAL EMPLOYMENT ADVISORY COUNCIL

Washington, D.C.

KF
3464
.L48
1982

Copyright 1982 by the Equal Employment Advisory Council
   1015 15th Street, N.W.
   Washington, D.C. 20005

   Library of Congress Catalog Card Number 82-84264
   International Standard Book Number 0-937856-06-1

All rights reserved. No part of this work may be reproduced or copied in any form or by any means without written permission of the publisher.

EEAC and the Monograph Series

The Equal Employment Advisory Council is a voluntary nonprofit association organized to promote the common interest of employers and the general public in the development and implementation of sound government policies and procedures pertaining to nondiscriminatory employment practices. The Council's membership comprises a broad segment of the employer community in the United States including both individual employers and trade associations. The members of EEAC are firmly committed to the principle of equal employment opportunity and to the goals of our nation's equal em-employment laws.

With the rapidly increasing volume of court and administrative rulings interpreting these laws, it is essential that those responsible for decisions in precedent-setting cases understand as fully as possible the practical impact of their decisions. It is the function of the Council to explain this impact and to suggest useful solutions through the filing of amicus curiae briefs in significant court proceedings and through submitting appropriate comments to administrative agencies.

In order to deal with particularly significant issues in greater depth, from time to time EEAC has also published resource books on compliance with EEO requirements. Occasionally, however, legal and policy issues arise that need immediate discussion but are neither ripe for direct EEAC amicus participation nor sufficiently developed to warrant book-length treatment. To provide our members and the public with timely analysis and discussion of such issues, the Council has established an EEAC Monograph Series.

Each title in the Monograph Series is devoted to a topic that is of current concern to EEO practitioners. In keeping with EEAC's longstanding emphasis on program content and utility, the monographs are designed to impart a maximum amount of information and analysis in a comparatively brief and readable form useful to both lawyers and non-lawyers responsible for dealing with equal employment matters. Like other EEAC publications, the underlying purpose of the series is to provide the employer community with resources that will assist compliance with the civil rights laws and enhance the quality of employer representation in the EEO area. More generally, we hope this and future monographs will assist EEAC member companies and others to better understand and prepare for changes in EEO law and policy.

FOREWORD

A growing number of employers have been involved in litigation in which management or supervisory personnel have been named as defendants in EEO suits challenging their business decisions. Many of these cases have yet to be decided, but experience has shown that allegations of personal liability not only have a chilling effect on supervisor morale, but may present obstacles to defense of the corporate EEO suit. The experience of these companies has also revealed a need for an easily obtainable analysis of available research material from which to craft a defense or become familiar with this undeveloped area of the law.

This Monograph has been prepared to provide such background material and to identify and analyze some of the issues and considerations that might arise when plaintiffs make personal liability claims against supervisors. Because it is an emerging issue, plaintiffs' theories are not yet fully developed, and the identification of appropriate defenses, to some degree, will have to await further legal developments. As the Monograph demonstrates, however, there is a substantial body of law that already has developed in this area. Furthermore, certain practical implications of personal supervisor liability suits for the corporation, for the individual supervisor and for corporate counsel also have become apparent.

Although these issues are discussed at length, we emphasize that the Monograph has been designed as an overview and not as an exhaustive treatment of the subject. In order to address specific situations that may arise for individual employers, the services of a lawyer or other expert assistance knowledgeable in this area of the law is recommended.

The primary drafting of the Monograph was performed by Daniel R. Levinson, a partner in the Washington, D.C., law firm of McGuiness & Williams. He is a graduate of Georgetown University Law School, and a member of the California, New York and District of Columbia Bars. Substantive and editorial suggestions were made by Robert E. Williams and Douglas S. McDowell, also partners in McGuiness & Williams. Mr. Williams is a member of the Illinois and D.C. Bars, and Mr. McDowell is a member of the Michigan and D.C. Bars.

The initial research and suggestions of Kevin S. McGuiness, Esq., are gratefully acknowledged.

Equal Employment Advisory Council

Washington, D.C.
November, 1982

TABLE OF CONTENTS

Page

FOREWORD v

I. INTRODUCTION AND OVERVIEW

A. Personal Supervisor Liability Issues Arise Most Often Where State Common Law Actions Are Brought as Part of EEO Lawsuits. 1

B. Caveat: Plaintiffs in Many EEO Suits Name Supervisors as Defendants for Reasons Other Than Obtaining Personal Liability. 4

II. PERSONAL SUPERVISOR LIABILITY UNDER EEO-SPECIFIC STATUTES

A. Title VII Focuses Upon Employer Conduct, and Neither the Statute nor Its Legislative History Authorizes Personal Supervisor Liability. 7

B. Like Title VII, The Age Discrimination In Employment Act Is Directed Toward Employers, And Courts Generally Have Been Unsympathetic To Personal Supervisor Liability Suits. 12

C. The Equal Pay Act Repeatedly Has Been Construed Not To Encompass Personal Supervisor Liability. 14

III. PERSONAL SUPERVISOR LIABILITY UNDER STATE TORT LAW AND SECTION 1981

A. Personal Supervisor Liability Allegations Occur Most Frequently In State Tort Claims Based On Assault, Defamation, Harassment, Etc. 16

B. State Tort Claims May Be Introduced In Federal Court By Being Appended To Federal Claims Under Title VII And Other EEO Statutes, Or Becoming An Integral Part Of A Federal Suit Under 42 U.S.C. § 1981.   17

IV. CORPORATE INDEMNIFICATION OF SUPERVISORS NAMED AS DEFENDANTS IN EEO SUITS

A. Significant Policy Considerations May Favor Corporate Indemnification Of Supervisors Named In EEO Suits.   25

B. State Laws Generally Permit At Least Some Degree Of Corporate Indemnification.   26

V. SPECIAL CONCERNS REGARDING PERSONAL SUPERVISOR LIABILITY IN THE PUBLIC SECTOR

A. 42 U.S.C. § 1983 Provides A Remedy Against State Officials Or Others Acting Under Color Of State Law Who Violate A Citizen's Rights As Secured By The Constitution And Laws.   30

B. Public Sector Officials Also May Be Subject To Liability Under Common Law Tort Or Constitutional Tort Law.   32

VI. CONCLUSION   36

VII. SAMPLE LETTERS ON CORPORATE INDEMNIFICATION POLICIES   37

INDEX OF AUTHORITIES   44

I. INTRODUCTION AND OVERVIEW

A. Personal Supervisor Liability Issues Arise Most Often Where State Common Law Actions are Brought as Part of EEO Lawsuits.

[In an effort to increase the possibility of recovery in EEO-related lawsuits, plaintiffs' counsel are broadening their suits to include novel theories. An increasingly-used strategy is to bring suit personally against corporate officers, managers or supervisors. Although courts have generally considered such actions unsupportable under employment discrimination statutes, which are directed toward employers, individual supervisor liability has been established in cases brought under state tort theories.]

Economic recession combined with a growing awareness by employees of legal rights and remedies are expanding the breadth of employment discrimination litigation in novel ways. Plaintiff-employees are reaching beyond established federal statutory protections to overcome some of the limitations of these laws and thus increase the possibility of obtaining legal relief.[1] Perhaps the best known example of this expansion concerns the erosion of the so-called "termination-at-will" doctrine in which a growing number of

---

[1] Federal laws that regulate employment practices include Title VII of the Civil Rights Act of 1964, 42 U.S.C. § 2000e, *et seq.* (1980); the National Labor Relations Act, 29 U.S.C. § 161, *et seq.* (1980); the Age Discrimination in Employment Act, 29 U.S.C. § 621 (1980) the Equal Pay Act, 29 U.S.C. § 206(d) (1980); The Rehabilitation Act, 29 U.S.C. §§ 601-794 (1980); and Executive Order No. 11246, 3 C.F.R. 169, *codified at* 42 U.S.C. § 2000e (1980).

Commentators have suggested the following reasons for plaintiffs seeking causes of action under state or common law instead of, or in addition to the remedies provided in these federal statutes:

> Since monetary damages under Title VII are limited to recovery of back pay, alternate causes of action under state law may be particularly important where the discriminatee might recover damages other than back pay. State causes of action may also be particularly important where there are jurisdictional barriers to proceeding under Title VII.
>
> * * *
>
> Additional considerations with respect to proceeding under these alternative causes of action are that either side may be entitled to a jury trial. Further, if recovery is possible under state law for sickness (*e.g.*, mental pain and suffering) or for defamation, it may be tax-free to the recipient, whereas back pay is fully taxable.

B. Schlei & P. Grossman, *Employment Discrimination Law* 678-79 (1976)(footnotes omitted).

courts are permitting employees to sue an employer for unlawful discharge even though no employment contract exists and no violation of federal or state anti-discrimination laws has been alleged.[2]

Although not as frequently discussed as the erosion of the "termination-at-will" doctrine, another disturbing feature in the expansion of EEO-related litigation is the growing number of lawsuits filed in which plaintiffs name individual supervisors as defendants for the purpose of obtaining recovery against them personally for alleged violations of what might be considered EEO-related rights. For example, in one case currently pending before a U.S. district court, a black female formerly employed by the defendant company is seeking to hold both the defendant company and her former supervisor liable for a series of unwanted verbal and physical sexual advances which she claims the supervisor made toward her.[3] Her Complaint alleges further that company managers were told about the incidents but failed to take any action, and that ultimately she was compelled to quit her job because of continued sexual harassment. The suit was brought against the company in federal court under Title VII. The Complaint in the case, however, also includes claims against the former supervisor personally for "assault and battery" and against her former supervisor and the company for "intentional infliction of emotional distress." The plaintiff seeks damages of $35,000 against the supervisor alone.

As in the complaint summarized above, most litigated claims involving personal supervisor liability do not arise under statutes like Title VII, which specifically prohibit employment discrimination. Indeed, in the comparatively few cases that have raised personal supervisor liability issues in the context of EEO-specific statutes, courts generally have refused to entertain such claims.[4] Rather, plaintiffs seek to impose personal supervisor liability using "com-

---

[2] The law generally does not guarantee or create any right to permanent employment. An increasing number of state courts, however, are construing the common law of their state to permit "wrongful discharge" suits based either on general notions of public policy or upon an implied promise of good faith and fair dealing. *See, e.g., Monge v. Beebe Rubber Co.*, 114 N.H. 130, 316 A.2d 549 (1974); *Fortune v. National Cash Register Co.*, 373 Mass. 96, 364 N.E.2d 1251 (1977). *See generally* Note, *Limiting The Right to Terminate at Will—Have The Courts Forgotten The Employer?* 35 Vanderbilt L. Rev. 201 (January 1982).

[3] Since the case has not yet been tried, names of the parties are omitted here to avoid any unnecessary adverse publicity.

[4] *See, e.g., Friend v. Union Dime Savings Bank*, 24 FEP Cases 1307 (S.D.N.Y. 1980) (ADEA); *Women in City Government, United v. New York*, 515 F. Supp. 295 (S.D.N.Y. 1981); and *Pate v. Transit District*, 21 FEP Cases 1227 (N.D. Cal. 1977) (Title VII). *But cf., Hanshaw v. Delaware Tech. & Community College*, 405 F. Supp. 292 (D. Del. 1975) (Title VII).

mon law"-type causes of actions, including a wide variety of torts. This is precisely the litigation strategy adopted by the plaintiff in the case above.

The law of "torts" (*i.e.*, civil wrongs) permits individuals to recover damages for a wide variety of personal injuries. Whether or not such wrongs are committed in the workplace, tort law typically permits recovery for assault and battery, defamation (libel or slander), interference with contractual relations, and the intentional infliction of emotional distress. Like "termination-at-will" cases,[5] these theories are based upon common law as construed by the various state courts.

The potential for lawsuits against supervisors based on tort theories, however, is not confined to state courts. As illustrated in the case above, Title VII plaintiffs in federal court may seek to attach state law claims related to their EEO action. *See Kyriazi v. Western Electric Co.*, 461 F. Supp. 894 (D. N.J. 1978), *aff'd*, 647 F.2d 388 (3d Cir. 1981). Similarly, under 42 U.S.C. § 1981, which states that "[a]ll persons . . . shall have the same right in every state . . . to make and enforce contracts . . . as is enjoyed by white citizens," and which secures the right to enter into contracts free from racial discrimination, *Johnson v. Railway Express Agency*, 421 U.S. 454, 459 (1975), courts may permit plaintiffs to allege against supervisors tortious interference with these contractual rights by bringing suit in federal court. *Manuel v. International Harvester Co.*, 502 F. Supp. 4577 (N.D. Ill. 1980)(black former employee may maintain action under § 1981 against two individual managers who allegedly determined that he would be terminated).

These tort-based cases, it may be argued, are not rooted in the principles of statutory employment discrimination law. Nevertheless, as the plaintiffs' bar increasingly explores new and sometimes novel theories to expand the possibilities of recovery for employee or applicant plaintiffs, corporations and their officers, managers and supervisors should be prepared to defend against EEO-related tort suits and the unique issues of liability they may raise.

As discussed in Part II of this Paper, under statutes dealing specifically with employment discrimination, enforcement agencies and the courts have generally accepted the proposition that individual officers, managers and supervisors are not subject to liability for decisions and actions they take in their capacity as agents of the corporation. The policy of holding only the corporation liable for actions by officers and supervisors is well recognized in federal statutory labor laws, having its roots in the National Labor Relations Act ("NLRA"). Individual liability traditionally has *not* been assessed under the NLRA. *See Friend v. Union Dime Savings Bank, supra*.

[5] *See* note 2, *supra*.

For analytic purposes, our discussion of personal supervisor liability case law has been divided into two major categories: EEO-specific statutes and common law theories. The first category (Part II of this Paper) will concentrate upon EEO statutes, that is, those laws that contain specific prohibitions against employment discrimination. These statutes have in common a specific designation of parties potentially liable for statutory violations, which includes, in each instance, "employers." As explained in detail below, under statutes dealing specifically with employment discrimination, enforcement agencies and the courts have generally accepted the proposition that individual officers, managers and supervisors are *not* subject to liability for decisions and actions they take in their capacity as agents of the corporation.

In Part III of this Paper, we will explore how personal supervisor liability issues have arisen in suits under state tort law and Section 1981. Under these laws, which are designed more generally to redress violations of civil or contract rights, plaintiffs have successfully established individual supervisor liability.

This Paper will also address some of the legal and policy concerns with respect to corporate indemnification of supervisors charged with personal liability. We will conclude with a discussion of the special legal provisions regarding personal supervisor liability in the public sector.

B. Caveat: Plaintiffs in Many EEO Suits Name Supervisors as Defendants for Reasons Other Than Obtaining Personal Liability.

> [Supervisors are often named in EEO lawsuits only for the purpose of establishing the ultimate liability of the employer-entity. Supervisors also may be named in EEOC charges only to help assure that they will be available for conciliation.]

Before examining the supervisor liability issue in detail, an important distinction in fair employment case law should be made. There are many employment discrimination cases in which plaintiffs name individual defendants *not* in anticipation of obtaining recovery against them personally, but for other, unrelated purposes. Because these cases may be confused with genuine personal liability cases, they are discussed below with emphasis upon the three most common situations under which they occur: (1) *alter ego* cases: (2) *respondeat superior* cases; and (3) procedural cases.

In *alter ego* cases, management representatives are named defendants, and may be held liable, because they have a substantial ownership interest in the business entity and thus may properly be considered "employers." *See, e.g., Marshall v. Arlene Knitwear Inc.*, 454 F. Supp. 715 (E.D.N.Y. 1978), *aff'd in part, rev'd in part on other grounds*, 608 F.2d 1369 (2d Cir. 1979)(ADEA Case); *EEOC v. Rinella and Rinella*, 401 F. Supp. 175 (N.D. Ill. 1975)(Title VII). Accordingly, these are not true personal supervisor liability cases but rather are examples of cases where supervisors may have such control of corporate activities that they, in fact, are owner-employers.

Under a second type of theory—*respondeat superior*—corporations are liable for the acts of their agents performed in the course of employment. Plaintiffs, therefore, sometimes name individual defendants only to help establish the ultimate liability of the employer. *See, e.g., Miller v. Bank of America*, 600 F.2d 211 (9th Cir. 1979)(Title VII); *Bundy v. Jackson*, 641 F.2d 934 (D.C. Cir. 1981)(Title VII). These are "principal-agent" cases in which liability is imputed to the employer and thus are not cases concerning personal supervisory liability. The wording used in some court opinions in this area, however, is sometimes obscure, and may incorrectly lead readers to assume that personal liability is in issue. A court may state in the course of its opinion, for example, that Title VII cases "typically contemplate liability for supervisor employees. . . ." *Guyette v. Stauffer Chemical Co.*, 518 F. Supp. 521 (D. N.J. 1981). As in the case cited, however, the court is simply defining the limits of the business entity's liability for the supervisor-employee conduct, and *not* indicating personal liability for the supervisor-employee.

Finally, plaintiffs may name individual defendants for procedural purposes related to assuring that those responsible for the company's EEO policies will be available for conciliation, or perhaps, for pre-trial discovery. In *Coley v. M&M Mars, Inc.*, 461 F. Supp. 1073 (M.D. Ga. 1978), for example, the court refused to dismiss personnel and plant managers even though not named in the EEOC charge, saying:

> This court's Title VII jurisdiction extends only to those defendants named in plaintiff's EEOC complaint. 42 U.S.C. § 2000e-5. Courts have liberally construed this requirement so as to include individuals who receive actual notice of the complaint and whose involvement in the EEOC conciliation process is reasonably necessary to adequately remedy the complaint's allegations.[6]

(See footnote on Page 6)

In sum, EEO cases that name individual supervisors as defendants are not necessarily *personal* liability situations, and the case law in this area should be read carefully to ascertain the plaintiff's purpose in naming individual defendants. In the great majority of cases brought under EEO-specific statutes, individual defendants are named for purposes other than obtaining personal liability.

---

[6] 461 F. Supp. at 1075. On this point, *Denny v. Westfield State College*, 25 FEP Cases 957 (D. Mass. 1981), notes the cases and theories under Title VII concerning the necessity for filing, or reasons for excusing the non-filing, of charges naming individuals. In *Denny*, the plaintiff filed an EEOC charge against the State College, and then in a Title VII suit named as defendants, among others, eleven individuals sued collectively as the Board of Trustees. The district court denied a motion to dismiss the suit as to the individual trustees, ruling that they were properly joined even though they were not named as respondents in the EEOC charge.

The court emphasized that the Board of Trustees "is the employer of faculty at state colleges, including the plaintiffs in this case." *Id.* at 962. No reference was made, however, to the imposition of personal liability. Rather, the court was concerned only with the procedural issue raised by the failure to name certain defendants as respondents in the EEOC charge.

II. PERSONAL SUPERVISOR LIABILITY UNDER EEO-SPECIFIC STATUTES

A. Title VII Focuses Upon Employer Conduct, and Neither the Statute nor Its Legislative History Authorizes Personal Supervisor Liability.

[Nothing in Title VII or its legislative history suggests that Congress contemplated personal supervisor liability. Furthermore, the term "employer" in the National Labor Relations Act has been construed *not* to encompass individual liability. Although there are few cases on the issue under Title VII, court opinions generally support the view that only an owner-employer is liable for Title VII violations.]

Title VII of the Civil Rights Act of 1964,[7] which prohibits employment discrimination on the basis of race, color, religion, sex and national origin, proscribes the conduct of three kinds of entities *only*: (1) employers; (2) employment agencies; and (3) labor organizations. The employer definition includes "any agent" of such an employer. There is substantial authority, however, for the proposition that the agency language does not expand the potential universe of employer-defendants to include employees who supervise EEO activities. Rather, the term merely defines the extent to which a business entity may be liable under Title VII for the conduct of employees acting in its behalf.

When required to construe the term "employer" in Title VII, federal courts have been hampered by the lack of legislative history. Some courts accordingly have turned to the legislative history of the National Labor Relations Act (NLRA).[8] The NLRA not only shares many legislative characteristics with Title VII,[9] but its history on the "employer" definition is more revealing.[10]

---

[7] 42 U.S.C. § 2000e, *et seq.* (1980).
[8] 29 U.S.C. § 161, *et seq.* (1980).
[9] *See, e.g., Ford Motor Co. v. EEOC*, 102 S. Ct. 3057, 3065-66 (1982); *Franks v. Bowman Transportation Co.*, 424 U.S. 747, 769 (1976) (NLRA and Title VII are "twin" areas of employment discrimination law).
[10] *See Guyette v. Stauffer Chemical Co.*, 518 F. Supp. 521, 523-24 (D. N.J. 1981); *Kidd v. American Air Filter Co.*, 23 FEP Cases 381 (W.D. Ky. 1980); *Smith v. Dutra Trucking Co.*, 410 F. Supp. 513, 515 (N.D. Cal. 1976), *aff'd mem.*, 580 F.2d 1054 (9th Cir. 1978), *cert. denied sub nom. Smith v. United States*, 439 U.S. 1079 (1979); and *Friend v. Union Dime Savings Bank*, 24 FEP Cases 1307, 1310 (S.D.N.Y. 1980) (ADEA case).

The original Wagner Act included in the definition of "employer" the phrase "any person acting *in the interest* of an employer" (emphasis added). The Board did not interpret the term to impose personal liability on supervisors. Sometimes, however, the Board "imputed to employers anything that anyone connected with an employer, no matter how remotely, said or did, notwithstanding that the employer had not authorized what was said or done, and in many cases even had prohibited it." HOUSE COMM. ON EDUCATION AND LABOR, LABOR-MANAGEMENT RELATIONS ACT, 1947, H. R. Rep. No. 245, 80th Cong., 1st Sess. 11 (1947), and cases cited therein. Accordingly, Congress changed the definition in 1947 to narrow the Act's scope so as to avoid employer responsibility for the misconduct of individuals who were remotely connected with the employer. The Taft-Hartley amendment, by defining as an "employer" "any person acting *as an agent* of an employer," made employers responsible only for what people said or did when it was within the actual or apparent scope of their authority. *Id.*

In keeping with this legislative history, cases decided under the NLRA have held that an employer's individual representatives are not personally liable for the payment of back pay to an employee who has been unlawfully discharged or discriminated against except where the management representative is actually the *alter ego* of the employer.[11] The Board has couched its rationale in terms of who controls employer assets solely against which a back pay award can run.[12]

The Equal Employment Opportunity Commission (EEOC), which is responsible for enforcement of Title VII, does not appear to have interpreted the term "employer" any more broadly than the NLRA's definition. Its procedural regulations simply refer to the statute's definition of an "employer." EEOC Proc. Reg. at 29 C.F.R. Part 1601.2. EEOC's *Compliance Manual* for its field representatives contains no indication of individual agent liability. *Manual* Section 2.7, entitled "Other Parties Named In Charge," states those circumstances when parties beside the "employer" should be named and mentions several "agent" relationships—unions, other employers as hiring referral sources, and trade associations—but not individuals. *Interpretive Manual* Section 155, entitled "Responsibility for Acts of Agents," refers only to the accountability of employers for acts of their agents.

---

[11] *See NLRB v. Operating Engineers Local 925*, 460 F.2d 589 (5th Cir. 1972); *Central Dispatch, Inc.*, 229 N.L.R.B. 979 (1977).
[12] *See Bon Hennings Logging Co.*, 132 N.L.R.B. 97, 98 (1964).

EEOC's emphasis upon employer responsibility for supervisor actions is further reflected in the Agency's sexual harassment regulations, which anticipate employer liability for supervisor actions but are silent with respect to supervisor liability, even where the supervisor acts contrary to employer policy. 29 C.F.R. Part 1604.11 (c), in pertinent part, states:

> Applying general Title VII principles, an employer, employment agency, joint apprenticeship committee or labor organization (hereinafter collectively referred to as "employer") is responsible for its acts and those of its agents and supervisory employees with respect to sexual harassment regardless of whether the specific acts complained of were authorized or even forbidden by the employer and regardless of whether the employer knew or should have known of their occurrence.

Accordingly, EEOC has confined its lawsuits to business entities, and does not name individual defendants.

There have been only a few private Title VII suits that have raised issues which may bear on personal supervisor liability questions. In private sector Title VII cases, courts have consistently addressed supervisor liability in terms of employer liability for the acts of supervisors and generally have not also held supervisors to be personally liable for their actions. "Generally speaking," the D.C. Circuit has declared, "an employer is chargeable with Title VII violations occasioned by discriminatory practices of supervisory personnel." *Barnes v. Costle*, 561 F.2d 983, 993 (1977). As the Ninth Circuit explained in *Silver v. KCA, Inc.*, 586 F.2d 138, 141 (1978), the "specific evil at which Title VII was directed was not the eradication of all discrimination by private individuals, undesirable though that is, but the eradication of discrimination by employers against employees." Such reasoning not only precludes employer liability for the acts of non-supervisory employees, but also may be relied upon to support the exclusion of personal liability under Title VII of supervisor-employees. Accordingly, in some sexual harassment cases, which often present factual situations that appear particularly appropriate for relieving employers of liability, courts have permitted plaintiffs alleging sexual harassment by supervisors to hold the employer entity solely liable for sex discrimination on the theory of *respondeat superior*.[13]

---

[13] *See Miller v. Bank of America*, 600 F.2d 211 (9th Cir. 1979); *Bundy v. Jackson*, 641 F.2d 934 (D.C. Cir. 1981). *But see Corne v. Bausch and Lomb, Inc.*, 390 F. Supp. 161 (D. Ariz. 1975), *vacated and remanded mem.*, 562 F.2d 55 (9th Cir. 1977), in

In the public sector, several courts that have addressed the issue directly have concluded that public personal supervisor liability under Title VII is inappropriate. In *Padway v. Palches*, 665 F.2d 965 (9th Cir. 1982), for example, an elementary school principal brought a Title VII suit alleging sex discrimination against the school superintendent and individual school board trustees. The court noted that a back pay award against the individual defendants was not available under Title VII:

> We note that 42 U.S.C. § 2000e [Title VII] speaks of unlawful practices by the employer, and not of unlawful practices by officers or employees of the employer. Back pay awards are to be paid by the employer. 42 U.S.C. § 2000e-5(g). The individual defendants cannot be held liable for back pay.

Id. at 968. *See also Snow v. Nevada Dept. of Prisons*, 29 FEP Cases 742 (D. Nev. 1982); *Clanton v. Orleans Parish School Bd.*, 649 F.2d 1084, 1099 n.19 (5th Cir. 1981)("our research has failed to uncover a single case in which a public official has been held personally liable for backpay under Title VII").[14] Similarly, in *Women in City Government, United v. New York*, 515 F. Supp. 295 (S.D.N.Y. 1981), the court held that trustees of a city's retirement system were not employers within the meaning of Title VII and therefore were not liable in their individual capacities for discrimination that may have occurred against female employees. And, in *Pate v. Transit District, et al.*, 21 FEP Cases 1227 (N.D. Cal. 1977), the court concluded that a personnel manager was not an employer within the terms of the Act, and therefore could not be held personally liable under Title VII for the unlawful practices of his employer.[15]

---

which the district court concluded that the "verbal and physical sexual advances" of a supervisor toward his female subordinates reflected only a "personal proclivity," which was unrelated to the nature of their employment and therefore not actionable under Title VII.

[14] The Fifth Circuit in *Clanton* agreed with the Second Circuit that there is "no statutory warrant for such an award against a public official" in his individual capacity. *Monell v. Department of Social Services*, 532 F.2d 259, 261 (2d Cir. 1976) (dictum), *rev'd on other grounds*, 436 U.S. 658 (1978). State and local governments, it should be noted, are fully subject to Title VII. It has been held, therefore, that a state agency that employs a supervisor who engages in discrimination is liable under Title VII for the supervisor's conduct. *Cleary v. Department of Public Welfare*, 21 FEP Cases 687 (E.D. Pa. 1979).

[15] *See also Beasley v. Griffin*, 427 F. Supp. 801 (D. Mass. 1977); *Brooks v. Brinegan*, 391 F. Supp. 720 (D. Okla. 1974). *Cf. Hutchison v. Lake Oswego School Dist. No. 7*, 519 F.2d 961 (9th Cir. 1975) ("qualified immunity" defense for individual government officials held applicable to Title VII cases).

Occasionally, however, courts have suggested the possibility of personal liability under Title VII. In *Hanshaw v. Delaware Tech. & Community College*, 405 F. Supp. 292 (D. Del. 1975), for example, plaintiffs alleged race and sex discrimination and sued both the employer college and board and college officials in their individual and official capacities. The court stated that because the college's board of trustees could act only through its members, and because the board's actions appeared to accord with the wishes of the individual members, individual liability under Title VII against the board members was appropriate. It should be noted, however, that at some points in its opinion, the court's language suggests that it was merely defining the extent of the college's liability. The individuals were to be kept in the suit, the court said, "if the Board members can be considered agents" of the public institution. *Id.* at 298. *See also Kelly v. Richland School Dist.*, 463 F. Supp. 216, 218 (D. S.C. 1978)(superintendent of school district is an agent of the employer under Title VII and can thus be "held accountable" for violations of the statute); *Raysor v. New York State Dept. of Health*, 29 E.P.D. ¶ 32,926 (S.D.N.Y. 1981)(middle-level executive who had recommended discharge of black employee for alleged race biased reasons potentially liable under Title VII).

Whatever the precedential value of *Hanshaw*, the outcome in that case is worth noting, for it suggests where liability may ultimately reside as a practical matter. According to the attorney who represented the individual defendants, that case was settled prior to trial without a finding of liability. Moreover, the insurance carrier for the *college* made payments to the plaintiffs as part of the settlement.

In sum, the weight of authority plainly supports the view that Title VII is strictly employer-oriented, and an unsuitable vehicle for personal supervisor liability lawsuits.

B. Like Title VII, The Age Discrimination In Employment Act Is Directed Toward Employers, And Courts Generally Have Been Unsympathetic To Personal Supervisor Liability Suits.

> [The prohibitions in the Age Discrimination In Employment Act are directed against employers which, as the district court explained in *Friend v. Union Dime Savings Bank*, would include only those who are "an integral part of the employer unit" and not simply individuals "working as employees."]

The prohibitions of the Age Discrimination in Employment Act[16] ("ADEA") are worded in a manner almost identical to Title VII, except that "age" replaces "race, color, religion, sex, and national origin." Covered employers, as in Title VII, include their "agents." Once again, however, the legislative history with respect to the agency language is silent.

Because of its similarity in coverage to Title VII, the question of individual supervisor liability under the ADEA warrants treatment similar to that under Title VII, which is to say, by reference to the NLRA. This, in fact, was done in *Friend v. Union Dime Savings Bank*, 24 FEP Cases 1307 (S.D.N.Y. 1980), with the result that individual suits under the ADEA against the defendant's corporate officers were dismissed.

Friend contains perhaps the clearest exposition of why individual supervisor liability for EEO-related decisions is inappropriate. The case involved an action under the ADEA against a bank and three officers and trustees of the bank. The court found that the legislative history of both the ADEA and Title VII were silent on the construction of the agency language in the two statutes, but relied on the NLRA and its legislative history to conclude that individual agent liability was not contemplated:

> From the legislative history it is clear that when Congress included 'any agent' in the NLRA it was an attempt to limit the employer's liability rather than to grant a new cause against all agents or employees of an employer.
>
> *Id.* at 1310.

The district court emphasized that the bank officers and trustees did not have a substantial financial interest in the bank so as to make them "an integral part of the employer unit." The court pointed out that the plaintiff received his salary and benefits from the cor-

---
[16] 29 U.S.C. § 621 (1980).

poration itself, not from the individual officers, and that the individual defendants "were working as employees on behalf of the bank and in the scope of their authority, and should not be held individually accountable." *Id.*

In another case, however, a district court permitted a plaintiff to use the ADEA as the basis for an alleged tort violation perhaps sufficient to hold a corporate officer individually liable despite the defendant acting at all times on behalf of the corporation. In *Zises v. Prudential Ins. Co.*, 25 FEP Cases 557 (D. Mass. 1981), a former employee brought a claim that he was discharged in Massachusetts because of his age in violation of the ADEA. Included as named defendants in the suits were two Prudential executives based out-of-state who were allegedly involved in the termination process. On a motion to dismiss claims against the individual defendants for lack of personal jurisdiction, the district court concluded that one of the defendants could be held liable on the basis of acts committed in Massachusetts on behalf of his corporate employer. Noting that Massachusetts law permitted the exercise of jurisdiction over those "causing tortious injury" in the state, the district court found that "[s]ince the ADEA creates a statutory duty on employers not to terminate employees under age 70 on the basis of age, and since a violation of the statute makes the employer liable in damages, I find that plaintiff's claim may properly be described as 'tortious injury' within the meaning" of Massachusetts law. *Id.* at 559.

While *Zises* is a procedural case, the court's reliance on tort theory to implicate a corporate employee individually in an otherwise purely federal ADEA suit could have disturbing substantive consequences. The suit was framed only in terms of a federal ADEA action, but in resolving the question of personal jurisdiction, the trial court introduced non-EEO cases for the purpose of establishing that an officer "is liable for torts in which he personally participated, whether or not he was acting within the scope of his authority." 25 FEP Cases at 559-60, *quoting Lahr v. Adell Chemical Co.*, 300 F.2d 256, 260 (1st Cir. 1962)(defamation). The court thus left open the possibility that plaintiffs could mix ADEA and tort claims and assert personal supervisor liability even though, as *Friend* makes plain, there is no support for such a reading in the federal statute.

C. The Equal Pay Act Repeatedly Has Been Construed Not To Encompass Personal Supervisor Liability.

> [Although the definition of "employer" under the Equal Pay Act includes any person acting directly or indirectly in the interest of an employer, courts have regularly dismissed Equal Pay Act claims as to individual defendants.]

The Equal Pay Act,[17] which prohibits employer pay discrimination based on sex, was passed as an amendment to the Fair Labor Standards Act of 1938 ("FLSA"), which regulates minimum wages, overtime, and child labor. Its coverage and exemption provisions differ substantially from Title VII and the ADEA.

On its face, the FLSA definition of an employer appears to be more inclusive of individuals than the definitions of employer under Title VII, the ADEA or the NLRA. The FLSA defines an "employer" as "any person acting directly or indirectly in the interest of an employer in relation to an employee. . . ." 29 U.S.C. § 203(d). Nevertheless, courts have regularly dismissed claims as to individual defendants even though they acted as agents of the employer. *See, e.g., Wertz v. Pure Ice Co.* 322 F.2d 259 (8th Cir. 1978)(court refused to find an individual liable for wages due employees despite his being a majority stockholder in the company); *Brinkley v. Department of Public Safety*, 22 FEP Cases 164, 166 (N.D. Ga. 1980)(employer easily identified and "no additional relief may be obtained from the individual defendants. . . ."); *Blowers v. Lawyers Coop. Pub. Co.*, 25 FEP Cases 1425 (W.D.N.Y. 1980)(employer's officials are not "employers" subject to Equal Pay Act). As one court noted in words that could apply with equal validity to most EEO-related corporate litigation:

> Examination of the work relationship properly focuses on the underlying economic realities. . . . In these circumstances no claim is made that the responsible entity is not plaintiff's employer or that the culpable party can be reached only by disengaging complicated inter- or intra-corporate concatenations. Easton, undoubtedly plaintiff's employer, remains available in this action for possible redress of plaintiff's injuries. No additional relief can be obtained from the individual defendants and no purpose will be served by retaining them in the litigation for the Equal Pay Act claims. (Citation omitted).

---

[17] 29 U.S.C. § 206(d) (1980).

Martin v. Easton Publishing Co., 478 F. Supp. 796, 799 (E.D. Pa. 1979).

In sum, attempts by plaintiffs to have personal liability imposed on supervisors under EEO-specific statutes generally are looked upon with disfavor by the courts. Most courts seem to agree that the prohibitions in employment discrimination laws apply only to business entities. Personal supervisor liability would be incongruous with statutory frameworks plainly designed to regulate the practices of *owner interests.*

III. PERSONAL SUPERVISOR LIABILITY UNDER STATE TORT LAW AND SECTION 1981

A. Personal Supervisor Liability Allegations Occur Most Frequently In State Tort Claims Based On Assault, Defamation, Harassment, Etc.

[Increasingly plaintiffs are invoking "common-law" type causes of action against employers and their supervisors. Most often, these claims will be based on tort theories, such as assault, defamation, or harassment. These claims, not rooted in the principles of statutory employment discrimination law, have been successfully pressed against corporate officers, managers and supervisors.]

A tort is an unlawful violation of a person's right created by law, for which the appropriate remedy is a common law action for damages by the injured person. The common law, as construed among various state courts, encompasses a wide range of tort theories, including assault and battery, defamation, interference with contractual relations and intentional infliction of emotional distress.[18]

As an integral part of the common law, these tort theories are generally a matter of state law, and their application will vary among state jurisdictions. Importantly, tort law usually applies equally in the workplace, and, as indicated earlier,[19] there are various reasons why plaintiffs may choose to invoke state tort law instead of, or in addition to, federal or state remedies under statutes specifically prohibiting employment discrimination. In particular, plaintiffs may invoke tort law to obtain personal liability against defendant supervisors.

For example, in *Alcorn v. Anbro Engineering, Inc.*, 2 Cal. 3d 493, 2 FEP Cases 712 (1970), the plaintiff alleged that he suffered physical illness, shock, nausea and insomnia after he was subjected to racial epithets and told he was fired by his supervisor, whose actions were subsequently confirmed and ratified by the employer. The California Supreme Court applied California tort law to rule that the plaintiff could maintain a cause of action against both the

---

[18] *See* W. Prosser, *Law of Torts* (4th ed. 1971).
[19] *See* note 1, *supra*.

employer and the supervisor for the intentional infliction of emotional distress. Citing the California Labor Code's recognition of equal employment opportunity as a civil right, the state supreme court emphasized that the employer and supervisor stood in positions of authority over the plaintiff. "Thus," the court stated, "plaintiff's status as an employee should entitle him to a greater degree of protection from insult and outrage than if he were a stranger to defendants." 2 FEP Cases at 714. *See also Campbell v. Ford Industries, Inc.*, 274 Ore. 243, 546 P.2d 141 (1976) (tort asserted against officers and directors of defendant firm for wrongful interference with employment). *But see Martin v. Platt*, 386 N.E.2d 1026, 1027 (Ind. App. 1979) (discharge by officers of firm held to be within their supervisory duties and not actionable).

An added dimension in this area is the increasing use of state tort claims to broaden traditional EEO suits brought under federal statutes in federal courts. As explained below, state tort claims not only may widen the ambit of potential employer liability, but may increase the "defendant pool" to include corporate officers, managers and supervisors who would otherwise not be subject to liability under EEO-specific statutes.

B. State Tort Claims May Be Introduced In Federal Court By Being Appended To Federal Claims Under Title VII And Other EEO Statutes, Or Becoming An Integral Part Of A Federal Suit Under 42 U.S.C. § 1981.

> [The potential for lawsuits against supervisors based on state tort theories is not confined to state courts. Title VII plaintiffs in federal court have been permitted in appropriate circumstances to attach state law claims. Furthermore, 42 U.S.C. § 1981, which secures the right to enter into contracts free from racial discrimination, may be invoked by plaintiffs in federal court to allege against supervisors tortious interference with these contractual rights.]

As stated earlier, tort law may provide an avenue of relief for plaintiffs who seek to hold supervisors personally liable for discriminatory conduct. Under the doctrine of pendent jurisdiction or the use of 42 U.S.C. § 1981, state tort theories increasingly are becoming a part of federal EEO lawsuits.[20]

---

[20] State tort suits may also be entertained in federal court under diversity-of-citizenship jurisdiction. 28 U.S.C. § 1332 (1980). If the citizenship of the plaintiff and

Litigants have brought state claims in federal court as part of a federal case under the doctrine of pendent jurisdiction. The doctrine may apply whenever the relationship between the federal and state claims is such that together they comprise what reasonable people would regard as but one "case," *i.e.*, where it would be logical to expect that the two would be litigated together. *United Mine Workers v. Gibbs*, 383 U.S. 715 (1966) (labor dispute which involved both federal law and a state claim of unlawful conspiracy; pendent jurisdiction of the latter was sustained).[21]

The extent to which state actions may properly be appended to Title VII federal court suits is a matter of court discretion applying the facts of particular cases to the standards set out by the Supreme Court in *UMW v. Gibbs*. Corporations and their supervisor defendants may argue, for example, that state tort claims are inconsistent with and would tend to subvert Title VII policies, rights and remedies; and, further, that tort claims will raise a variety of legal theories and issues which will predominate over the federal claims and tend to confuse a jury.

Some courts have been sympathetic to the problems raised for defendants by Title VII-tort suit combinations. In *Kiss v. Tamarac Utilities, Inc.*, 463 F. Supp. 951 (S.D. Fla. 1978), the district court in a Title VII suit declined to exercise pendent jurisdiction over the plaintiff's claims for damages under state law for defamation, in-

---

defendant is different and the matter in controversy exceeds $10,000, a state-created cause of action may be brought in federal court even though the case involves no federally-created rights at all.

Since a corporation for diversity purposes is deemed a citizen of its state of incorporation *and* a citizen of the state where it has its principal place of business, diversity-based suits do not often arise in the employment context because the citizenship of the plaintiff-employee and defendant employer typically is the same.

In *Rogers v. Loew's L'Enfant Plaza Hotel*, 29 FEP Cases 828 (D.D.C. 1981), however, a former employee brought a tort action against her employer and supervisor for alleged sexual harassment. Her common-law tort claims, based on the right to privacy, assault and battery and the infliction of emotional distress were allowed to be heard in federal court solely through diversity-of-citizenship jurisdiction.

[21] In deciding whether to hear state claims, a federal court looks to considerations of judicial economy, convenience and fairness to the litigants, whether the federal claims had been dismissed before trial, whether the state issues predominate, and the likelihood of jury confusion in treating divergent legal theories of relief. *Compare Guyette v. Stauffer Chemical Co.*, 518 F. Supp. 521 (D. N.J. 1981) (sexual harassment theory of recovery under Title VII bears distinct similarities to, and to a large extent arises out of, common law torts such as assault and battery and intentional interference with contractual relations; pendent state claim allowed), *with Ferguson v. Mobil Oil Corp.*, 443 F. Supp. 1334 (S.D.N.Y. 1978), *aff'd mem.*, 607 F.2d 995 (2d Cir. 1979) (postdischarge "blacklisting" claim not cognizable as a Title VII act of discrimination or as pendent state claim).

terference with employment relationships and assault. The court observed that:

> [T]he relief which Congress has provided under Title VII is equitable in nature. Congress has thus impliedly expressed a policy disfavoring the award of compensatory and punitive damages in employment discrimination cases.... In contrast, the state-law claims...are claims based on alleged intentional torts for which plaintiff seeks to recover both compensatory and punitive damages. Apart from its effect on the power of this Court to exercise jurisdiction over the 'pendent parties,' this factor is one which militates against the exercise of the court's discretion to hear pendent claims, since the pendent claims 'might well become the predominant claims because of the monetary damages sought.'
>
> * * *
>
> A procedural factor against the exercise of pendent jurisdiction...is the unavailability of trial by jury under Title VII, whereas the Plaintiff is entitled to a jury trial on the tort claims....[22]

Often, however, courts have permitted state claims to be appended to federal EEO statutorily-based actions.[23] In a number of

---

[22] 463 F. Supp. at 954 (citations omitted). Other courts that have declined, in Title VII actions, to exercise pendent jurisdiction over state law claims, include *Ferguson v. Mobil Oil Corp.*, 443 F. Supp. 1334 (S.D.N.Y. 1978), *aff'd mem.*, 607 F.2d 995 (2d Cir. 1979) (Title VII and "blacklisting" claims did not derive from a common nucleus of operative facts); *Gerlach v. Michigan Bell Telephone Co.*, 448 F. Supp. 1168 (E.D. Mich. 1978) (substantial differences in the nature of the factual inquiries required under the state and federal claims and the inconsistency of the remedies requested under the state and federal claims); *Van Hoomissen v. Xerox Corp.*, 368 F. Supp. 829 (N.D. Cal. 1973) (pendent state claim for intentional infliction of emotional distress is inconsistent with and beyond scope of Title VII claim).

[23] *See, e.g., Kelly v. American Standard, Inc.*, 640 F.2d 974 (9th Cir. 1981) (state action for emotional distress appended to ADEA action); *Pittman v. Grand Trunk Western R.R. Co.*, 17 FEP Cases 870 (E.D. Mich. 1978) (pendent claims under Michigan Civil Rights Act and for relief for discharge in contravention to public policy allowed in addition to Title VII and § 1981 claims); *Fellows v. Medford Corp.*, 431 F. Supp. 199 (D. Ore. 1977) (in ADEA action pendent jurisdiction allowed for "new tort of employee discharge based on a socially undesirable motive" with compensatory and possibly punitive damages). A U.S. district court in Maryland recently observed, however, that "[t]he majority of Federal Courts which have dealt with the question of whether emotional distress claims should be appended to Title VII actions have held that they should not." *Clark v. J.M. Benson Co.*, 30 E.P.D. ¶ 33,046 at 27,058 (D. Md. 1982), *citing Hughes v. Marsh Instrument Co.*, 27 E.P.D. ¶ 32,333 (N.D. Ill. 1981), and cases cited therein.

such cases, individual supervisors have been sued. Many of these cases involve alleged incidents of sexual harassment.

In *Kyriazi v. Western Electric Co.*, 461 F. Supp. 894 (D. N.J. 1978), *aff'd*, 647 F.2d 388 (3d Cir. 1981), for example, a female former employee brought a sexual harassment claim under Title VII to which was appended state law claims against five individual defendants for having tortiously interfered with plaintiff's employment relationship. The individual defendants included both supervisors and co-workers. In addition to finding the employer liable under Title VII on a variety of individual and class claims, the court upheld the state claims. The court found that evidence that plaintiff's male co-workers jointly agreed to ridicule and harass her as an obese woman, and that her supervisors chose to overlook that action, demonstrated that the co-workers and the supervisors had maliciously interfered with her employment contract under New Jersey law. "Where one intentionally acts to deprive another of an economic benefit, including an employment relationship," the court declared, "the law of New Jersey confers a right of action on the party aggrieved." *Id.* at 950.[24]

---

[24] Although technically not a personal supervisor liability case, the court's opinion in *Clark v. World Airways, Inc.*, 24 E.P.D. ¶ 31,385 (D. D.C. 1980), is instructive on how courts distinguish EEO and tort claims. The case involved a sexual harassment suit brought by a female former employee against a corporation and its president and principal owner. The plaintiff alleged that the corporation president had made sexual advances toward the plaintiff which she rebuffed and which forced her to resign. The action against the corporation consisted of three claims: (1) a Title VII claim for sexual harassment of the plaintiff by the corporation president; (2) a claim of negligence in the supervision of the president by the corporation; and (3) a claim of sexual assault by the president for which the corporation was responsible. She also alleged that the president was personally liable for committing the common law torts of extortion and interference with contract.

The court dismissed the tort claims against the president. The court found no tort of extortion to exist. With respect to the tort action based on contractual interference, the court identified three defects: (1) the president's breach of the obligations he owed his own company could not be the basis for the tort—the interference must be that of a third party; (2) the doctrine of wrongful interference with contract appears inapplicable with respect to a contract terminable at will; and (3) recognition of such a tort is generally confined to situations in which the defendant seeks to reap commercial advantage from his wrong.

The court also dismissed the Title VII claim against the corporation on the ground that the evidence showed that corporation and president never made submission to the sexual advances a term or condition of employment. The court did let stand, however, a $52,000 judgment against the corporation based on the sexual assault claim. The court found ample evidence from which the jury could conclude that the president sexually assaulted the plaintiff, and that while doing so he was serving his employer.

In *Kyriazi*, the court was careful to delineate between EEO statutory and state tort issues.[25] These concepts inevitably become intertwined, however, in suits brought in federal court under 42 U.S.C. § 1981. Although not by its terms an employment discrimination statute, Section 1981 encompasses prohibitions against race discrimination in employment in a way that permits the introduction of state tort law.

Section 1981 (a part of the Civil Rights Act of 1866) bars intentional race discrimination in several protected areas.[26] Most § 1981 cases, however, have concerned the right "to make and enforce contracts," including employment contracts. *See e.g., Johnson v. Railway Express Agency, Inc.*, 421 U.S. 454 (1975); *Jones v. Alfred H. Mayer*, 392 U.S. 409, 442 n.78 (1968) ("the right to contract for employment [is] a right secured by 42 U.S.C. § 1981"); *Bethel v. Jendoco Construction Corp.*, 570 F.2d 1168 (3d Cir. 1978). Since Section 1981 is not an EEO-specific statute, however, the specific focus on employer conduct explicit in EEO statutes is absent. As the sampling of cases below indicates, one result has been that some

---

[25] Not all courts in pendent jurisdiction cases distinguish as carefully between federal and state causes of actions. In *Cancellier v. Federated Dept. Stores*, 672 F.2d 1312 (9th Cir. 1982), *cert. denied*, 51 U.S.L.W. 3256 (U.S. Oct. 4, 1982), the court of appeals ruled that the ADEA does not preempt an award of tort damages on pendent state claims. Although it is not a personal supervisor liability case, the court's decision is particularly disturbing because it let stand the failure of the trial judge to break down the verdict between age discrimination and state law claims. The court conceded, however, that:

> When state claims for breach of the implied covenant of good faith and fair dealing are joined to claims of age discrimination under the ADEA . . . review of jury verdicts presents special difficulty to appellate courts. A general verdict may conceal punitive damages which may not be allowed under the ADEA. If the state claims are flawed, the entire verdict may have to be reversed. For these reasons, a separate verdict for each claim and a separate verdict on punitive damages is strongly preferred.

Id. at 1317.

[26] 42 U.S.C. § 1981 states:

> All persons within the jurisdiction of the United States shall have the same right in every State and Territory to make and enforce contracts, to sue, be parties, give evidence, and to full and equal benefit of all laws and proceedings for the security of persons and property as is enjoyed by white persons, and shall be subject to like punishment, penalties, taxes, licenses, and exactions of every kind, and to no other.

The statute proscribes *only* racial discrimination, *Runyon v. McCrory*, 427 U.S. 160, 167 (1976), but covers both blacks and whites. *McDonald v. Santa Fe Trail Transportation Co.*, 427 U.S. 273, 285-87 (1976). The Supreme Court recently held that liability may not be imposed under Section 1981 without proof of intentional discrimination. *General Building Contractors Assn. v. Pennsylvania*, 102 S. Ct. 3141 (1982).

plaintiffs have had greater success in expanding the "defendant pool" in employment discrimination cases to include officers and executives.

Individual director liability under Section 1981 was recognized in *Tillman v. Wheaton-Haven Recreation Ass'n, Inc.*, 517 F.2d 1141 (4th Cir. 1975). The court in *Tillman* concluded that an action brought under Section 1981 is "fundamentally for the redress of a tort." *Id.* at 1143.[27] The court thus held that directors of a nonprofit corporation which operated a swimming pool and denied admission to blacks were personally liable for their actions.

Whether supervisors are subject to individual liability in EEO suits under Section 1981 will depend in part upon how courts construe the statute's contract requirement and its relationship to applicable state tort law regarding tortious interference with contract rights. In *Willis v. Safeway Stores*, 17 FEP Cases 102 (N.D. Tex. 1978), for example, a black female employee who had been demoted brought suit under Section 1981 against both the employer and its employee relations manager. Finding that Section 1981 by its terms requires the existence of a contract, the court granted the employee manager's motion to dismiss. Because there was no contract between the plaintiff and the employee relations manager, no Section 1981 claim against the manager was cognizable. The court made no reference to any tort-based theory. *Cf. Leslie v. Philadelphia 1976 Bicentennial Corp.*, 332 F. Supp. 83 (E.D. Pa. 1971) (no § 1981 liability could attach to individuals who had not assumed any personal obligations with respect to plaintiff's employment with the corporation).

On the other hand, in *Garcia v. Rush-Presbyterian St. Luke's Medical Center*, 80 F.R.D. 254 (N.D. Ill. 1978), the district court permitted a Mexican-American plaintiff to sue hospital officials under Section 1981. The court acknowledged that "technically defendant Rush [Hospital] is the employer in a position to contract with plaintiffs," but that the individual defendants were the executive officers "who formulate and execute the employment policies" al-

---

[27] In support of its conclusion, the court cited *Curtis v. Loether*, 415 U.S. 189 (1974). In *Curtis*, a fair housing case brought under Title VIII of the 1964 Civil Rights Act, Justice Marshall, expressing the views of a unanimous Supreme Court, likened damage actions brought under the statute to tort suits, and declared that either party was thus entitled on demand to a jury trial. In approaching the jury trial issue under Title VIII, Justice Marshall quoted C. Gregory & H. Kalven, *Cases and Materials on Torts* 961 (2d ed. 1969), for the proposition that "under the logic of the common law development of a law of insult and indignity, racial discrimination might be treated as a dignitary tort." 415 U.S. at 195 n.10.

leged to be discriminatory. The court concluded that "a third party's interference with rights guaranteed under [§ 1981] will subject such a person to personal liability."

To the same effect is *Manuel v. International Harvester Co.*, 23 FEP Cases 1477 (N.D. Ill. 1980). There the plaintiff, a black male, brought suit under Section 1981 against his employer and two individual employees "who determined that plaintiff would be terminated from his position...." *Id.* at 1480. The court denied a motion to dismiss the individual suits, concluding that Section 1981 permits suit "against both corporations and corporate directors or officers who authorize, direct, or participate in the alleged discriminatory conduct."

Finally, in *Hernandez v. Erlenbusch*, 368 F. Supp. 752 (D. Ore. 1973), the district court ruled favorably for plaintiffs in a Section 1981-1983 action against the owners and bartender in a tavern which had a policy of precluding foreign language from being spoken at the bar. The bartender had helped enforce the discriminatory policy. In assessing damages against the defendants, the court made no distinction between the tavern owners and the bartender.

State governments and state officials are subject to liability under Section 1981. *Burkey v. Marshall County Bd. of Ed.*, 513 F. Supp. 1084 (N.D. W.Va. 1981). Most EEO-based Section 1981 suits are brought against institutions, since a valid Section 1981 claim runs to the party with whom plaintiffs' contractual rights have been impaired. *See Stewart v. Hannon*, 469 F. Supp. 1142 (N.D. Ill. 1979). In *Faraca v. Clements*, 506 F.2d 956 (5th Cir.), *cert. denied*, 422 U.S. 1006 (1975), however, the court permitted a Section 1981 claim against the state-appointed director of a health facility based on tortious interference with the right to contract. In that case, the defendant had refused to employ the plaintiff as an administrator because he did not believe one who is part of a racially mixed couple should assume such a position. The court concluded that the defendant could be held personally liable under Section 1981 for compensatory damages.[28]

In sum, corporate managers and supervisors are most likely to confront personal supervisor liability suits based on state tort theory,

---

[28] It should be noted that many public sector cases involve individual officers for purposes only of establishing a principal-agent relationship, much like the private sector cases discussed above. *See, e.g., Bradley v. Rockland City Mental Health Center*, 25 FEP Cases 225 (S.D.N.Y. 1980); *Cleary v. Department of Public Welfare*, 21 FEP Cases 687 (D. Pa. 1979); *Vanguard Justice Society v. Hughes*, 471 F. Supp. 670 (D. Md. 1979); *Harbart v. Rapp*, 419 F. Supp. 6 (W.D. Okla. 1976); *Padilla v. Stringes and City of Alburquerque*, 395 F. Supp. 495 (D. N.M. 1974).

either as presented in a state tort claim or as made an integral part of a suit under Section 1981. One method of protecting supervisors against some of these lawsuits is through corporate indemnification programs. The next section will examine some of the more significant legal and policy issues bearing on the indemnification question.

IV. CORPORATE INDEMNIFICATION OF SUPERVISORS NAMED AS DEFENDANTS IN EEO SUITS

A. Significant Policy Considerations May Favor Corporate Indemnification Of Supervisors Named In EEO Suits.

[EEO managers who perform their responsibilities in good faith should be encouraged to carry out duties and obligations with confidence, secure that their employer will protect them against any attempts by unsuccessful job applicants or disenchanted employees to single them out in EEO-related litigation. A corporate indemnification policy encourages the close cooperation among executives necessary to formulate and implement properly EEO policy.]

Indemnification includes the reimbursement by one of the loss or damages suffered by another. In *In re E.C. Warner Co.*, 232 Minn. 207, 45 N.W.2d 388 (1950), the Minnesota Supreme Court identified three policy reasons why a corporation might indemnify directors named in a lawsuit: (1) to encourage innocent directors to resist unjust charges and provide them an opportunity to hire competent counsel; (2) to induce responsible businessmen to accept the post of director; and (3) to discourage in large measure stockholders' litigation. These reasons are easily, and quite properly, adaptable to supervisors named in lawsuits in the EEO area. EEO managers who act on behalf of their employer in good faith should be encouraged to accept responsibility and should be protected against possible attempts by job applicants or employees to single out a supervisor to undertake the burdens of litigation.

Other practical reasons for corporate indemnification exist as well. Both the formulation and execution of corporate EEO policy is a complicated task that depends upon the collaboration of many individuals. This need for cooperation may be seriously compromised if supervisory personnel believe they may be exposed to personal liability when they act in good faith to make what they believe to be lawful employment-related decisions on behalf of the company. Obviously, such a situation may irreparably damage morale, and, by forcing supervisors in self-defense to second-guess the company, invite confusion among management ranks.

B. State Laws Generally Permit At Least Some Degree Of Corporate Indemnification.

> [Depending upon state law, indemnification may include expenses, settlements, judgments and fines, if the company official acted in good faith and reasonably believed he was serving the best interests of the corporation. Questions may still arise, however, over the permissibility of liability insurance to protect against possible EEO violations. Also, it should be anticipated that a lawyer's dual representation of a corporation and its supervisor may raise conflict-of-interest issues.]

The courts in Delaware, where many Fortune 500 companies are incorporated, have indicated that "directors are entitled to rely on the honesty and integrity of their subordinates until something occurs to put them on suspicion that something is wrong. If such occurs and goes unheeded, then liability of the directors might well follow."[29] The public corporation and its directors, officers and managers confront such a complicated array of regulation, legislation and common law liability, however, that it is often difficult to judge when "suspicious" activity occurs such as to require corrective action. To help protect corporate management from liability arising from these judgment calls, many states permit corporate indemnification and authorize indemnification insurance. Depending upon the law of the state in which the company is incorporated, indemnification may include expenses, settlements, judgments and fines, if the company official acted in good faith and reasonably believed he was serving the best interests of the corporation.

In jurisdictions that permit indemnification, questions may arise over the use of liability insurance to protect against corporate and individual liability in connection with third party actions involving corporate executives. These issues are particularly complex in the EEO area, where important public policy considerations may impact upon the permissibility of otherwise appropriate corporate insurance arrangements. It is well settled that "[a] contract of insurance to indemnify a person for damages resulting from his own intentional misconduct is void as against public policy and the courts will not construe a contract to provide such coverage." *Industrial Sugars, Inc. v. Standard Accident Insurance Co.*, 338 F.2d 673, 676 (7th Cir. 1964).

---

[29] *Graham v. Allis-Chalmers Manufacturing Co.*, 41 Del. Ch. 78, 188 A.2d 125, 130 (1963). *See also Burks v. Lasker*, 441 U.S. 471 (1979); *Gall v. Exxon*, 418 F. Supp. 508 (S.D.N.Y. 1976).

In *Solo Cup Co. v. Federal Insurance Co.*, 619 F.2d 1178 (7th Cir. 1980), *cert. denied*, 449 U.S. 1033, for example, the employer sued the issuer of an umbrella excess liability policy seeking indemnity for legal fees and sums paid in settlement of a class action employment discrimination suit. Under the policy, the insurer had a duty to defend and indemnify the insured against occurrences *unintentionally* resulting in personal injury, defined as including discrimination. Noting that a Title VII plaintiff may establish a violation under either a disparate treatment or a disparate impact theory, the court of appeals observed that proof of discriminatory motive is critical in the former but unnecessary in the latter.[30] The Court thus construed the policy to include coverage of disparate impact liability and held that the disparate impact claim which could have been proved under the allegations of the underlying complaint was a claim potentially within the coverage of the policy.

The insurer in *Solo Cup* had argued that the public policy against employment discrimination embodied in Title VII prohibited insurance coverage of disparate impact liability. The court of appeals, *id.* at 1188, rejected the assertion:

> We do not think that allowing an employer to insure itself against losses incurred by reason of disparate impact liabilities will tend in any way to injure the public good, which we equate here with that equality of employment opportunity mandated by Title VII. To the contrary, the fact of insurance may be helpful toward achieving the desirable goal of voluntary compliance with the Act. The statistical proofs in disparate impact actions, most particularly those involving employment testing, have become increasingly complex and employers now often retain batteries of experts to validate their selection criteria. Such complex analyses of employment standards, while apparently necessary in order to ensure that an employer's policies do not needlessly place a stumbling block in the way of women or minorities, may well become, as a practical matter, beyond the financial capabilities of all but the largest employers. The involvement of insurance in the field might, however, ease the burden on the smaller employer by making claim prevention services available

---

[30] The disparate impact theory, the court of appeals explained, is employed in Title VII suits to analyze the validity of employment practices which are fair and neutral in form, but discriminatory in operation.

on a cost effective basis to help employers evaluate their employment standards. Workmen's compensation insurers have, by way of analogy, no doubt helped prevent numerous employee injuries, and it is not undesirable, nor inconceivable, that discrimination insurers might aid in preventing the injury of discrimination as well.[31]

Other courts which have concluded that insurance policies covered employment discrimination settlements include *Union Camp Corp. v. Continental Casualty Co.*, 452 F. Supp. 565 (S.D. Ga. 1978) (protection against losses resulting from discriminatory practices not violative of public policy); *Transport Insurance Co. v. Lee Way Motor Freight*, 487 F. Supp. 1325 (N.D. Tex. 1980); *Legg Mason Wood Walker v. INA*, 23 FEP Cases 778 (D. D.C. 1980) (noting, however, that an insurance policy covering intentional discrimination would likely violate public policy and thus be unenforceable). *See generally* Willborn, *Insurance, Public Policy And Employment Discrimination*, 66 Minn. L. Rev. 1003 (July 1982).

Another important consideration in indemnification lawsuits is the issue of dual representation. A lawyer's simultaneous representation of a corporation and its defendant-supervisor may raise conflict-of-interest issues. For example, the company may wish to settle and the supervisor may want to litigate, perhaps to "clear" a reputation, particularly in cases alleging sexual harassment. If corporate counsel is expected to represent individual supervisor defendants, the consent of the supervisor defendant should be obtained and the proceedings monitored closely should the interests of the company and the supervisor in fact diverge.[32]

---

[31] *Cf. Appalachian Ins. Co. v. Liberty Mut. Ins. Co.*, 676 F.2d 56 (3d Cir. 1982). This case also concerned the question of whether a liability insurer must provide coverage under an umbrella liability policy for losses its insured incurred in the settlement of class action litigation involving sex discrimination. The Third Circuit held that the insurance policy was not applicable in the case before it because the discrimination found *pre-dated* the effective date of the insurance policy.

The Third Circuit noted in its opinion that the insurer "did not contend that its policy excluded claims based on sex discrimination." *Id.* at 59. In a footnote, however, the court recounted that the insurer alleged in its complaint that indemnification was excluded under the terms of the policy because the injuries suffered by the class were the foreseeable result of the insured's intentional and deliberate acts. The Third Circuit declined to address the contention, stating that "[t]he district court did not reach this issue and neither do we." *Id.* at 59 n.6.

[32] The Code of Ethics of the American Bar Association requires that the professional judgment of a lawyer must be exercised solely for the benefit of his client, free of compromising influences and loyalties, and this precludes his acceptance of employment that will adversely affect his judgment or dilute his loyalty. Model Code of Professional Responsibility Canon 5. The Code also acknowledges, however, that [a]

On the basis that jurisdictions in which they are incorporated permit at least a limited degree of corporate indemnification, attached to this monograph are form letters that have been used by two companies to explain their indemnification policy to supervisors named as defendants in company-related lawsuits. (See Part VII, *infra.*) These letters are intended to serve as examples, and it is recognized that each corporation would have to determine whether similar letters would carry out its corporate indemnification policy.

---

lawyer may represent several clients whose interests are not actually or potentially differing. *Id.* at EC 5-19. See *Glueck v. Jonathan Logan*, 512 F. Supp. 223 (S.D.N.Y. 1981), *aff'd*, 653 F.2d 746 (2d Cir. 1981) (law firm's representation of incorporated trade association in multi-employer collective bargaining negotiations precludes, on conflict of interest grounds, firm's representation of discharged executive in his suit against employer-member of trade association).

V. SPECIAL CONCERNS REGARDING PERSONAL SUPERVISOR LIABILITY IN THE PUBLIC SECTOR

A. 42 U.S.C. § 1983 Provides A Remedy Against State Officials Or Others Acting Under Color Of State Law Who Violate A Citizen's Rights As Secured By The Constitution And Laws.

[Section 1983 is generally directed at constitutional deprivations caused by official state action or neglect by state officials. Such individuals may be held individually liable. Courts have ruled that state law determines whether supervisors may be held liable under Section 1983 for the misconduct of supervised employees.]

The primary purpose of this Paper is to examine the question of personal *corporate* supervisor liability under EEO law. There exist many public sector EEO cases, however, in which officials have been named as individual defendants in suits brought under laws not applicable to the private sector. Some of these cases, as well as the special provisions and principles of public sector law, are discussed below to distinguish this area from our primary topic and, at the same time, make readers aware of this related area of the law.

42 U.S.C. § 1983, along with the conspiracy statute that now appears at 42 U.S.C. § 1985,[33] was originally enacted as § 1 of the Civil Rights Act of 1871, also known as the Ku Klux Klan Act. By its terms,[34] Section 1983, which is designed to enforce the guarantees

---

[33] Section 1985(3), 42 U.S.C. § 1985(3)(1980), which prohibits conspiracies to deprive persons of their civil rights, encompasses suit against state and local officials in their individual capacities. *See, e.g., Glasson v. City of Louisville* 518 F.2d 899 (6th Cir.), *cert. denied*, 423 U.S. 930 (1975); *Bosely v. City of Euclid*, 496 F.2d 193 (6th Cir. 1974); *Curran v. Portland Superintending School Comm.*, 435 F. Supp. 1063 (D. Me. 1977). In *Great American Federal Savings & Loan Assn., et al. v. Novotny*, 442 U.S. 366 (1979), however, the Supreme Court held that Section 1985(3) could not be invoked to redress violations of Title VII.

[34] Section 1983 provides, in pertinent part, that:

> Every person who, under color of any statute, ordinance, regulation, custom, or usage of any State or Territory or the District of Columbia, subjects, or causes to be subjected, any citizen of the United States or other person within the jurisdiction thereof of the deprivation of any rights, privileges, of immunities secured by the Constitution and laws, shall be liable to the party injured in an action at law, suit in equity, or other proper proceeding for redress. . . .

to due process and equal protection under the Fourteenth Amendment, reaches only persons acting under color of state law. Accordingly, the statute does not reach purely private conduct, nor does it reach generally the conduct of federal agencies and officials.

Section 1983 has been used to reach employment discrimination involving police and fire departments, public schools, colleges and universities, public and semipublic hospitals, and state agencies.[35] It has long been construed to give a remedy to parties deprived of constitutional rights, privileges and immunities by an official's *abuse* of his position.[36] Accordingly, courts have held that state officials may well be individually liable in damages for their discriminatory conduct.[37]

It should be noted, however, that individual government officials typically enjoy at least a "qualified immunity" from personal monetary liability, so that compensatory awards against them may be appropriate only if they have "acted with such disregard of clearly established constitutional rights that [their] action cannot reasonably be characterized as being in good faith." *Wood v. Strickland*, 420 U.S. 308, 322 (1975).[38]

Several courts have held that whether supervisors may be held liable under Section 1983 for the misconduct of supervised employees

---

[35] *See* cases listed in Schlei & Grossman, *supra* note 1, at 615 nn.44-49.

[36] *See Monroe v. Pape*, 356 U.S. 167 (1961); *Williams v. United States*, 341 U.S. 97 (1951); *Screws v. United States*, 325 U.S. 91 (1945); *United States v. Classic*, 313 U.S. 299 (1941). In *Monell v. Department of Social Services*, 436 U.S. 658 (1978), the Supreme Court ruled that municipalities may be sued under Section 1982 for both damages and punitive relief.

[37] *See O'Brien v. Galloway*, 362 F. Supp. 901 (D. Del. 1973) (discharged town policeman's complaint alleging bad-faith deprivation of his constitutional rights by town police commissioner while acting under color of his authority and as member of board of commissioners and by mayor under color of his authority as mayor and as member of board stated cause of action against officials *individually* under Section 1983). *See also Donovan v. Reinbold*, 433 F.2d 739 (9th Cir. 1970); *Familias Unidas v. Briscoe*, 619 F.2d 391 (5th Cir. 1980); *Burt v. Board of Trustees*, 13 FEP Cases 1740 (4th Cir. 1975); *Wells v. Hutchinson*, 25 E.P.D. ¶ 31,689 (E.D. Tex. 1980).

[38] *See Axup v. Wade*, 28 FEP Cases 1045 (C.D. Cal. 1981). Some public officials, like judges, enjoy an absolute immunity from liability for acts done in the performance of their duties. *See, e.g., Bradley v. Fisher*, 13 Wall. 335 (U.S. 1872); *Imbler v. Pachtman*, 424 U.S. 409 (1976).

In *Owen v. City of Independence*, 445 U.S. 662 (1980), the Supreme Court stated that regardless of the benign or good-faith intention of the officers through which it acts, a local governmental entity sued under Section 1983 may not assert a good faith immunity defense. On the basis of *Owen*, the Fifth Circuit recently concluded that actions for damages against a party in his *official capacity* are, in essence, actions against the government entity of which the officer is an agent, and therefore government officials sued in their official capacity may not then assert good faith immunity as a defense in a § 1983 suit. *Universal Amusement Co., Inc. v. Hofheinz*, 646 F.2d 996 (5th Cir. 1981).

depends on state law. In *Hesselgesser v. Reilly*, 440 F.2d 901 (9th Cir. 1971), for example, the court found that county sheriffs were liable for civil rights violations perpetrated by their deputies while serving as jailers. The court relied upon Washington state statutes which provided that sheriffs shall be liable for negligence and misconduct of their jailers and other deputies. *See also Tuley v. Heyd*, 482 F.2d 590, 594 (5th Cir. 1973); *Scott v. Vandiver*, 476 F.2d 238, 241-43 (5th Cir. 1973).[39]

B. Public Sector Officials Also May Be Subject To Liability Under Common Law Tort Or Constitutional Tort Law.

> [Nothwithstanding statutory limitations and the absolute or qualified immunization of certain potential defendants, courts have occasionally held public officials liable under either common law tort or a "constitutional tort" theory.]

As with the expansion of EEO lawsuits in the private sector to include tort-based claims, plaintiffs in the public sector are increasingly pressing for court acceptance of tort theories to hold government officials and supervisors individually liable for employment discrimination. These efforts have met with limited success, both in the common law tort area and through the emerging body of law known as "constitutional torts."

As indicated earlier, government officials ordinarily enjoy at least a qualified immunity from personal monetary liability. Furthermore, public sector employees may be restricted by statute to certain remedies. For example, the Supreme Court has ruled that Title VII establishes the exclusive remedy for federal employment discrimination. *Brown v. GSA*, 425 U.S. 820 (1976). Accordingly, the Fifth Circuit has concluded that Title VII preempts suit by a federal employee under Section 1981 against a federal official in his

---

[39] The "color of state law" requirement under Section 1983 does not necessarily require a plaintiff to pinpoint a specific state statute. The district court held in *Athanas v. Board of Ed. School Dist. 111*, 28 FEP Cases 569 (N.D. Ill. 1980), for example, that a teacher who claimed he was an alcoholic and that he was discharged by the school district in violation of the Rehabilitation Act of 1973 could sue the school principal under Section 1983 for allegedly accusing the teacher of smelling of alcohol and demanding that he take a blood test that proved negative, where such accusations were accompanied by harassment, intimidation and coercion. It should be noted, however, that it is questionable whether the court correctly ruled that alcoholics are protected under Section 504 of the Rehabilitation Act either by case law or pertinent government regulations.

individual capacity. *See Newbold v. U.S. Postal Service*, 614 F.2d 46, 47 (1980), *cert. denied*, 449 U.S. 878.

Some courts have found, however, that in some circumstances neither statutory restrictions upon EEO remedies nor public sector immunity doctrines insulate public officials and supervisors from tort suits. In *Stewart v. Thomas*, 29 E.P.D. ¶ 32,860 (D.D.C. 1982), for example, a public employee, alleging sexual harassment, brought suit against her agency, the EEOC, under Title VII, and against her supervisor on the common law theories of assault, battery, "outrage," and intentional infliction of emotional distress. The EEOC supervisor moved to dismiss the tort claims against him on the ground, among other grounds, that the exclusive remedies for plaintiff's complaints lie under Title VII. The district court denied the defendant's motion, ruling that plaintiff's allegation of physical assault, "a highly personal violation beyond the meaning of discrimination," is separately actionable.[40] *Id.* at 26,059. The court found *Brown* inapposite to the case, stating that:

> It is clear that *Brown* prohibits deliberately bypassing Title VII, but it is also logical that, despite the defendant's contention, *Brown* does not prohibit federal employees who allege employment discrimination from suing on any cause of action arising from the same facts. For example, federal employees are permitted as a matter of course to bring suit under both Title VII and the Equal Pay Act. [Citations omitted.] The acts are to be construed in harmony and thus 'the same facts may form the basis for redress under both [statutes] if the requirements of each are separately satisfied and the claimant does not reap overlapping relief for the same wrong.' [Citations omitted.] The common law torts alleged here, like the problem of unequal pay, are distinct from the wrongs redressed by Title VII and this plaintiff should not be prevented from pursuing separate remedies.

Id. at 26,059.

In addition to liability under common law tort, public officials and supervisors also may be liable for committing "constitutional torts." In *Bivens v. Six Unknown Named Agents of the Federal Bu-*

---

[40] The court dismissed the claim based on "outrage" as redundant of the claim of intentional infliction of emotional distress. The court also ordered that to the extent that the plaintiff's claimed emotional injuries are alleged to have resulted from a stressful work environment rather than from assaultive behavior, her claim for intentional infliction of emotional distress was dismissed as subsumed by Title VII.

reau of Narcotics, 403 U.S. 388 (1971), the Supreme Court authorized damage actions against individual federal officials for infringement of Fourth Amendment rights. Most relevant in the context of employment discrimination are causes of action brought under the First, Fifth and Fourteenth Amendments.[41] In discussing this area, it should be noted that the Constitution provides limitations for the most part on *governmental* action and does not apply to actions by private individuals or corporations. See *United States v. Price*, 383 U.S. 787, 799 (1966); and *Sheila Rendell-Baker v. Sandra Kohn*, 102 S. Ct. 2764 (1982). Accordingly, the concept of a constitutional tort is limited to conduct of government officials.

Examples of such constitutional tort cases brought against public officials include *Yiamouyiannis v. Chemical Abstracts Service*, 521 F.2d 1392, 1399 (6th Cir. 1975), *cert. denied*, 439 U.S. 983 (1978)(First Amendment cause of action available to biochemist who was placed on probation because of speeches he made in opposition to the use of flourides in drinking water which were identified with his federally-funded employer); *Davis v. Passman*, 442 U.S. 228 (1979) (female employee of congressman discharged because of her sex, could sue under the Fifth Amendment for damages in the form of back pay); *Gentile v. Wallen*, 562 F.2d 193 (2d Cir. 1977) (denial of tenure and discharge of school teacher held to support a claim for Fourteenth Amendment violation of due process).

The use of *Bivens*-type actions is limited in several ways,[42] most

---

[41] The First Amendment provides that:

> Congress shall make no law respecting an establishment of religion, or prohibiting the free exercise thereof; or abridging the freedom of speech, or of the press; or the right of the people peaceably to assemble, and to petition the Government for a redress of grievances.

The Fifth Amendment, in pertinent part, provides that:

> No person shall . . . be deprived of life, liberty, or property, without due process of law. . . .

The Fourteenth Amendment, in pertinent part, provides that:

> No State shall make or enforce any law which shall abridge the privileges or immunities of citizens of the United States; nor shall any State deprive any person of life, liberty, or property, without due process of law; nor deny to any person within its jurisdiction the equal protection of the laws.

[42] A plaintiff who seeks to recover damages in a *Bivens*-type action must establish the following:

(1) that plaintiff's own constitutionally protected right was involved;

(2) that defendant's conduct violated that right according to the standards set forth in the relevant case law;

(3) that plaintiff has no effective means other than the judiciary to enforce that right; and

particularly by procedural limitations on remedies under Title VII[43] and the immunity doctrines discussed earlier. *See Butz v. Economou*, 438 U.S. 478 (1978).[44] In any event, public supervisors are subject to suit on constitutional tort grounds only if they participated in the alleged misconduct. *See Kite v. Kelley*, 546 F.2d 334, 337-38 (10th Cir. 1976); *Black v. United States*, 534 F.2d 524, 527-28 (2d Cir. 1976).

---

(4) that there is no explicit congressional declaration denying recovery and there are no "special factors counselling hesitation." *See Davis v. Passman*, 442 U.S. 288 (1979).

[43] *See* discussion of *Brown v. GSA*, 425 U.S. 820 (1976), *supra*, p. 31.

[44] Cases holding government officials not personally liable for back pay under the Fourteenth Amendment, after applying the qualified immunity standards of *Wood v. Strickland*, 420 U.S. 308, 322 (1975), include *Shirley v. Chagrin Falls Exempted Schools*, 521 F.2d 1329 (6th Cir. 1975), *cert. denied*, 424 U.S. 913 (1976); *Buck v. Board of Educ.*, 10 E.P.D. ¶ 10,363 (E.D.N.Y. 1975).

VI. CONCLUSION

Over fifteen years of litigation experience with a variety of federal statutes prohibiting employment discrimination demonstrates that in instances in which employer-defendants are found to have violated the law, it generally is the business owner or corporate entity alone that has been held liable. EEO-specific statutes plainly are designed to regulate employer conduct, and personal supervisor liability under such laws is inappropriate, as some courts have had occasion to so hold.

Personal supervisor liability is far more likely under state tort theories based on the common law or under 42 U.S.C. § 1981, which involves federal contract-related claims. Adults are personally liable for committing torts (like assault, battery, defamation, infliction of emotional distress) regardless of whether they occur in the workplace. EEO plaintiffs in federal court increasingly are attaching these state law claims to hold both employer and supervisor liable for alleged employment-related wrongs. Corporations and their upper-level personnel should be prepared to address the legal and policy questions that may arise when supervisor liability is alleged.

Corporate indemnification, in accordance with state law provisions, affords a method for protecting supervisors against harassing lawsuits. Significant public and corporate policy considerations, however, may require an ad hoc approach to indemnification based on the nature of the case.

Finally, it should be noted that many of the tort cases reviewed in this Paper concern outrageous instances of alleged sexual misconduct. These cases do not raise the subtle or technical issues characteristic of most Title VII litigation. Accordingly, supervisors generally need not anticipate the possibility of personal liability when engaged in good faith EEO compliance efforts. Tort cases should not overshadow the reality reflected in the general rule that it is the corporation, and not its supervisors, which is exposed to liability under Title VII and the EEO statutes. Thus, while it is well for supervisors to be aware of the possibility of personal liability in the event they engage in irresponsible conduct that results in injury to employees, this possibility should be kept in perspective and should not deter the full, good faith exercise of supervisory authority and discretion.

VII. SAMPLE LETTERS OF CORPORATE INDEMNIFICATION POLICIES

The following form letters have been used by two companies to explain their indemnification policy to supervisors named as defendants in company-related lawsuits. These letters are intended to serve as examples, and it is recognized that each corporation would have to determine whether similar letters would carry out its corporate indemnification policy.

LETTER ADDRESSED TO EMPLOYEE

We have been advised of the above cases in which you are named as a defendant. Based upon what we know about the cases at this time, it appears appropriate for the Company to advance the costs associated with the defense of your interests in each case. The Company policy is based upon applicable law and the Company's By Laws.

_____ By Laws provide for indemnification of an employee by the Company, including judgment, settlement and costs directly or separately attributable to his or her representation, if the President or his delegate determines that the employee acted in good faith and in a manner he reasonably believed to be in or not opposed to the best interests of the Company in the matter that is the subject of the lawsuit. In appropriate cases, costs of legal representation may be advanced by the Company before final disposition of the case, provided the employee involved promises to repay such costs if it is determined at a later time by the President or his delegate that the employee did not act in good faith.

On July _____ President of _____ issued a delegation of authority concerning indemnification of legal expenses of employees. He authorized an Executive Vice President or Senior Vice President to advance $15,000 in reasonable expenses. At this time, only approval of that amount is being requested. In the event the expenses are greater than that amount and it continues to appear that you are entitled under the Company policy to have the Company pay for your expenses, a further request for approval will be made.

The Company lawyer handling this matter is _____, telephone _____. He will be pleased to discuss it with you or with your attorney.

We will be pleased to handle payment of attorney fees on your behalf directly with the attorney, if you wish. Subject to these matters, we will advance such costs attributable to your legal representation in this case, provided you agree to repay promptly all such advancements if it is later determined that you are ineligible under the "good faith" standard to have such costs paid by the Company.

Therefore, if you desire to have the Company pay for your legal defense as described in this letter, in consideration thereof, please sign a copy of this letter and return it to me.

Very truly yours,

Litigation Department

Attachment

This will affirm my good faith belief that I have met the standard of conduct necessary for indemnification by the Company as set forth above. Further, I agree to repay to _____ all costs paid on my behalf in defense of this case if it is determined by the President or his delegate at any time that I am not entitled to have such costs paid by the Company as set forth above.

_____   _____
Employee   Date

MEMORANDUM

To: John Doe
From: James Law
Subject: Roe v. XYZ Corporation, John Doe, et al.

    This is to advise you that XYZ Corporation has selected the law firm of Wright & Wright to defend it in the suit filed by Richard Roe, and is prepared to provide the services of that firm to defend you as well, at its expense. Should you wish to retain counsel of your own choice you are, of course, free to do so. However, because we feel the Wright firm is well qualified to prepare the necessary defense and because there are obvious economies in preparing and coordinating the defense of the Corporation and the individual defendants through a single law firm, we will not look favorably upon advancing fees to you for the purpose of employing other counsel.

    If you desire to be defended by the Wright firm at XYZ's expense, please sign and return a copy of the Repayment Agreement to me. This Agreement provides (as required by Article VIII, Section 3, of XYZ's Bylaws, a copy of which is attached) that you will repay the cost of your defense by Wright & Wright in the unlikely event that it is ultimately determined that you are not entitled to indemnification.

    In the latter connection, you should note that you are entitled to full indemnification for attorneys' fees, court costs, judgments under, or amounts paid in settlement of, the Roe case if a court or independent legal counsel determines that you acted in good faith for a purpose which you reasonably believed to be in, or not opposed to, the best interest of XYZ, and note further that the mere termination of the case by judgment or settlement does not create a presumption that you did not act in good faith.

    It is possible that the Wright firm will represent all employes who are defendants in Roe, and it may be difficult to allocate their fees and expenses precisely among defendants if that should ever become necessary. Therefore, we have provided in the Repayment Agreement that, if necessary, you will pay XYZ for your share, determined on a fair and equitable basis, of the total resulting charges from joint representation. We will arrange with Wright & Wright to pay their charges directly.

    If you have any questions concerning this memorandum or the case, please do not hesitate to contact me.

                                        James Law
                                        General Counsel

I acknowledge receipt of a copy of this memorandum.

_____
        John Doe

Date: _____

REPAYMENT AGREEMENT

If it should be ultimately determined that I am not entitled to indemnification by XYZ for advances hereunder, I agree to repay XYZ by payroll deduction which I hereby expressly authorize, or otherwise, my share, determined on a fair and equitable basis, of legal charges described above and also any advances made to me or on my behalf on an individual basis.

                                           _____

                                                Date: _____

Section 3. Indemnification of Directors, Officers and Employes

(a) The Corporation (XYZ) may indemnify every person, his heirs, executors and administrators against any and all judgments, fines, amounts paid in settlement and reasonable expenses, including attorney's fees, incurred by him in connection with any claim, action, suit or proceeding (whether pending or threatened, brought by or in the right of XYZ or otherwise, civil, criminal, administrative or investigative, including appeals), to which he may be or is made a party by reason of his being or having been a director, officer or employe of XYZ (including any corporation merged into XYZ), or at XYZ's request of any other corporation in which XYZ owns or owned shares of capital stock or of which XYZ is a creditor.

(b) There shall be no indemnification, however, in the case of any criminal action or proceeding in relation to matters as to which such person shall be adjudged to have had reasonable cause to believe that his conduct was unlawful.

(c) Any such person who shall be or shall have been a Director, officer or employe of XYZ shall be entitled to indemnification as of right (i) if he has been wholly successful, on the merits or otherwise, with respect to any claim, action, suit or proceeding or (ii) in respect of matters as to which a court or independent legal counsel, approved by the XYZ Board, shall have determined that he acted in good faith for a purpose which he reasonably believed to be in or not opposed to the best interests of XYZ or such other corporation and, in addition, in the case of any criminal action or proceeding, had no reasonable cause to believe that his conduct was unlawful. Such court or independent counsel shall have the power to determine that such Director, officer or employe is entitled to indemnification as to some matters even though he is not so entitled as to others. The termination of any claim, action, suit, or proceeding by judgment, settlement, conviction or upon a plea of nolo contendere or its equivalent, shall not in itself create a presumption that any such Director, officer or employe did not act in good faith for a purpose which he reasonably believed to be in or not opposed to the best interests of XYZ and, in the case of any criminal action or proceeding that he had reasonable cause to believe that his conduct was unlawful.

(d) Amounts paid in indemnification shall include, but shall not be limited to, reasonable counsel and other fees and disbursements, and judgments, fines or penalties against, and amounts paid in settlement by, such Director, officer or employe. XYZ may advance expenses to, or where appropriate may itself at its expense undertake the defense of, any such Director, officer or employe provided that he shall have undertaken to repay or to reimburse such expenses if it should be ultimately determined that he is not entitled to indemnification under this article.

(e) Payments of indemnification made pursuant to this article shall be reported to the stockholders in the next proxy statement or otherwise, except that no such payments need be reported if such Director, officer or employe has been wholly successful on the merits or otherwise.

(f) The provisions of this article shall be applicable to all claims, actions, suits or proceedings, whether arising from acts or omissions to act occurring before or after the adoption hereof by the Board.

(g) The indemnification provided in this article shall not be exclusive of any rights to which any such Director, officer or employe may otherwise be entitled by contract or as a matter of law.

(h) If any portion of this article or any award of indemnification made hereunder shall for any reason be determined to be invalid, the remaining provisions hereof shall not otherwise be affected thereby but shall remain in full force and effect.

INDEX OF AUTHORITIES

Cases: *Page*

Alcorn v. Anbro Engineering, Inc., 2 Cal. 3d 493, 2 FEP Cases 712 (1970)	16
Appalachian Ins. Co. v. Liberty Mut. Ins. Co., 676 F.2d 56 (3d Cir. 1982)	28
Athanas v. Board of Ed. School Dist. 111, 28 FEP Cases 569 (N.D. Ill. 1980)	32
Axup v. Wade, 28 FEP Cases 1045 (C.D. Cal. 1981)	31
Barnes v. Costle, 561 F.2d 983 (D.C. Cir. 1977)	9
Beasley v. Griffin, 427 F. Supp. 801 (D. Mass. 1977)	10
Bethel v. Jendoco Construction Corp., 570 F.2d 1168 (3d Cir. 1978)	21
Bivens v. Six Unknown Named Agents of the Federal Bureau of Narcotics, 403 U.S. 388 (1971)	33, 34
Black v. United States, 534 F.2d 524 (2d Cir. 1976)	35
Blowers v. Lawyers Coop. Pub. Co., 25 FEP Cases 1425 (W.D.N.Y. 1980)	14
Bon Hennings Logging Co., 132 N.L.R.B. 97 (1964)	8
Bosely v. City of Euclid, 496 F.2d 193 (6th Cir. 1974)	30
Bradley v. Fisher, 13 Wall. 335 (U.S. 1872)	31
Bradley v. Rockland City Mental Health Center, 25 FEP Cases 225 (S.D.N.Y. 1980)	23
Brinkley v. Department of Public Safety, 22 FEP Cases 164 (N.D. Ga. 1980)	14
Brooks v. Brinegan, 391 F. Supp. 720 (D. Okla. 1974)	10
Brown v. GSA, 425 U.S. 820 (1976)	32, 33, 34
Buck v. Board of Educ., 10 E.P.D. ¶ 10,363 (E.D.N.Y. 1975)	35
Bundy v. Jackson, 641 F.2d 934 (D.C. Cir. 1981)	5, 9
Burkey v. Marshall County Bd. of Ed., 513 F. Supp. 1084 (N.D. W.Va. 1981)	23
Burks v. Lasker, 441 U.S. 471 (1979)	26
Burt v. Board of Trustees, 521 F.2d 1201 (4th Cir. 1975)	31
Butz v. Economou, 438 U.S. 478 (1978)	35
Campbell v. Ford Industries, Inc., 274 Ore. 243, 546 P.2d 141 (1976)	17

Cancellier v. Federated Dept. Stores, 672 F.2d 1312
(9th Cir. 1982), *cert. denied*, 51 U.S.L.W. 3256
(U.S. Oct. 4, 1982) 21
Central Dispatch, Inc., 229 N.L.R.B. 979 (1977) 8
Clark v. J. M. Benson Co., 30 E.P.D. ¶ 30,046 (D.
Md. 1982) 19
Clark v. World Airways, Inc., 24 E.P.D. ¶ 31,385
(D.D.C. 1980) 20
Cleary v. Department of Public Welfare, 21 FEP
Cases 687 (E.D. Pa. 1979) 10, 23
Clanton v. Orleans Parish School Bd., 649 F.2d
1084 (5th Cir. 1981) 10
Coley v. M&M Mars, Inc., 461 F. Supp. 1073 (M.D.
Ga. 1978) 5
Corne v. Bausch and Lomb, Inc., 390 F. Supp. 161
(E.D. Ariz. 1975), *vacated and remanded mem.*,
562 F.2d 55 (9th Cir. 1977) 9
Curran v. Portland Superintending School Comm.,
435 F. Supp. 1063 (D. Me. 1977) 30
Curtis v. Loether, 415 U.S. 189 (1974) 22
Davis v. Passman, 442 U.S. 228 (1979) 34, 35
Denny v. Westfield State College, 461 F. Supp. 1073
(D. Mass. 1981) 6
Donovan v. Reinbold, 433 F.2d 739 (9th Cir. 1970) 31
EEOC v. Rinella and Rinella, 401 F. Supp. 175
(N.D. Ill. 1975) 5, 31
Familias Unidas v. Briscoe, 619 F.2d 391 (5th Cir.
1980) 31
Faraca v. Clements, 506 F.2d 956 (5th Cir.), *cert.
denied*, 522 U.S. 1006 (1975) 23
Fellows v. Medford Corp., 431 F. Supp. 199 (D.
Ore. 1977) 19
Ferguson v. Mobil Oil Corp., 443 F. Supp. 1334
(S.D.N.Y. 1978) 18, 19
Fortune v. National Cash Register Co., 373 Mass.
96, 364 N.E.2d 1251 (1977) 2
Ford Motor Co. v. EEOC, 102 S. Ct. 3057 (1982) 7
Franks v. Bowman Transportation Co., 424 U.S.
747 (1976) 7
Friend v. Union Dime Savings Bank, 24 FEP
Cases 1307 (S.D.N.Y. 1980) 2, 3, 7, 12, 13
Gall v. Exxon, 418 F. Supp. 508 (S.D.N.Y. 1976) 26

Garcia v. Rush-Presbyterian St. Luke's Medical Center, 80 F.R.D. 254 (N.D. Ill. 1978)   22

General Building Contractors Assn. v. Pennsylvania, 102 S.Ct. 3141 (1982)   21

Gentile v. Wallen, 562 F.2d 193 (2d Cir. 1977)   34

Gerlach v. Michigan Bell Telephone Co., 448 F. Supp. 1168 (E.D. Mich. 1978)   19

Glasson v. City of Louisville, 518 F.2d 899 (6th Cir.), *cert. denied*, 423 U.S. 930 (1975)   30

Glueck v. Jonathan Logan, 512 F. Supp. 223 (S.D.N.Y. 1981), *aff'd*, 653 F.2d 746 (2d Cir. 1981)   29

Graham v. Allis-Chalmers Manufacturing Co., 41 Del. Ch. 78, 188 A.2d 125 (1963)   26

Great American Federal Savings & Loan Assn., et al. v. Novotny, 442 U.S. 366 (1979)   30

Guyette v. Stauffer Chemical Co., 518 F. Supp. 521 (D. N.J. 1981)   7, 18

Hanshaw v. Delaware Tech. & Community College, 405 F. Supp. 292 (D. Del. 1975)   2, 11

Harbart v. Rapp, 419 F. Supp. 6 (W.D. Okla. 1976)   23

Hernandez v. Erlenbusch, 368 F. Supp. 752 (D. Ore. 1973)   23

Hesselgesser v. Reilly, 440 F.2d 901 (9th Cir. 1971)   32

Hughes v. Marsh Instrument Co., 27 E.P.D. ¶ 32,333 (N.D. Ill. 1981)   19

Hutchison v. Lake Oswego School Dist. No. 7, 519 F.2d 961 (9th Cir. 1975)   10

Imbler v. Pachtman, 424 U.S. 409 (1976)   31

Industrial Sugars, Inc. v. Standard Accident Insurance Co., 338 F.2d 673 (7th Cir. 1964)   26

In re E.C. Warner Co., 232 Minn. 207, 45 N.W.2d 388 (1950)   25

Johnson v. Railway Express Agency, 421 U.S. 454 (1975)   3, 21

Jones v. Alfred H. Mayer, 392 U.S. 409 (1968)   21

Kelly v. American Standard, Inc., 640 F.2d 974 (9th Cir. 1981)   19

Kelly v. Richland School Dist., 463 F. Supp. 216 (D. S.C. 1978)   11

Kidd v. American Air Filter Co., 23 FEP Cases 381 (W.D. Ky. 1980)   7

Kiss v. Tamarac Utilities, Inc., 463 F. Supp. 951 (S.D. Fla. 1978)	18
Kite v. Kelley, 546 F.2d 334 (10th Cir. 1976)	35
Kyriazi v. Western Electric Co., 461 F. Supp. 894 (D. N.J. 1978), *aff'd*, 647 F.2d 388 (3d Cir. 1981)	3, 20
Lahr v. Adell Chemical Co., 300 F.2d 256 (1st Cir. 1962)	13
Legg Mason Wood Walker v. INA, 23 FEP Cases 778 (D.D.C. 1980)	28
Leslie v. Philadelphia 1976 Bicentennial Corp., 332 F.Supp. 83 (E.D. Pa. 1971)	22
Manuel v. International Harvester Co., 502 F. Supp. 45 (N.D. Ill. 1980)	3, 23
Marshall v. Arlene Knitwear Inc., 454 F. Supp. 715 (E.D.N.Y. 1978), *aff'd in part, rev'd in part on other grounds*, 608 F.2d 1369 (2d Cir. 1979)	5
Martin v. Easton Publishing Co., 478 F. Supp. 796 (E.D. Pa. 1979)	15
Martin v. Platt, 386 N.E.2d 1026 (Ind. App. 1979)	17
McDonald v. Santa Fe Trail Transportation Co., 427 U.S. 273 (1976)	21
Miller v. Bank of America, 600 F.2d 211 (9th Cir. 1979)	5, 9
Monell v. Dept. of Social Services, 436 U.S. 658 (1978)	10, 31
Monge v. Beebe Rubber Co., 114 N.H. 130, 316 A.2d 549 (1974)	1
Monroe v. Pape, 356 U.S. 167 (1961)	31
Newbold v. U.S. Postal Service, 614 F.2d 46 (5th Cir. 1980), *cert. denied*, 449 U.S. 878	33
NLRB v. Operating Engineers Local 925, 460 F.2d 589 (5th Cir. 1972)	8
O'Brien v. Galloway, 362 F. Supp. 901 (D. Del. 1973)	31
Owen v. City of Independence, 445 U.S. 662 (1980)	31
Padilla v. Stringes and City of Albuquerque, 395 F. Supp. 495 (D. N.M. 1974)	23
Padway v. Palches, 665 F.2d 965 (9th Cir. 1982)	10
Pate v. Transit District, 21 FEP Cases 1227 (N.D. Cal. 1977)	10
Pittman v. Grand Trunk Western R.R. Co., 17 FEP Cases 870 (E.D. Mich. 1978)	19

Raysor v. New York State Dept. of Health, 29
   E.P.D. ¶ 32,926 (S.D.N.Y. 1981)   11
Rogers v. Loew's L'Enfant Plaza Hotel, 29 FEP
   Cases 828 (D.D.C. 1981)   18
Runyon v. McCrory, 427 U.S. 160 (1976)   21
Scott v. Vandiver, 476 F.2d 238 (5th Cir. 1973)   32
Screws v. United States, 325 U.S. 91 (1945)   31
Sheila Rendell-Baker v. Sandra Kohn, 102 S. Ct.
   2764 (1982)   34
Shirely v. Chagrin Falls Exempted Schools, 521
   F.2d 1329 (6th Cir. 1975), *cert. denied*, 424 U.S.
   913 (1976)   35
Silver v. KCA, Inc., 586 F.2d 138 (9th Cir. 1978)   9
Smith v. Dutra Trucking Co., 410 F. Supp. 513
   (N.D. Cal. 1976), *aff'd mem.*, 580 F.2d 1054 (9th
   Cir. 1978), *cert. denied sub nom. Smith v. United
   States*, 439 U.S. 1079 (1979)   7
Snow v. Nevada Dept. of Prisons, 29 FEP Cases
   742 (D. Nev. 1982)   10
Solo Cup Co. v. Federal Insurance Co., 619 F.2d
   1178 (7th Cir. 1980), *cert. denied*, 449 U.S. 1033   27
Stewart v. Hannon, 469 F. Supp. 1142 (N.D. Ill.
   1979)   23
Stewart v. Thomas, 29 E.P.D. ¶ 32,860 (D. D.C.
   1982)   33
Tillman v. Wheaton-Haven Recreation Ass'n, Inc.,
   517 F.2d 1141 (4th Cir. 1975)   22
Transport Insurance Co. v. Lee Way Motor Freight,
   487 F. Supp. 1325 (N.D. Tex. 1980)   28
Tuley v. Heyd, 482 F.2d 590 (5th Cir. 1973)   32
Union Camp Corp. v. Continental Casualty Co.,
   452 F. Supp. 565 (S.D. Ga. 1978)   28
United Mine Workers v. Gibbs, 383 U.S. 715 (1966)   18
United States v. Classic, 313 U.S. 299 (1941)   31
United States v. Price, 383 U.S. 787 (1966)   34
Universal Amusement Co., v. Hofheinz, 646 F.2d
   996 (5th Cir. 1981)   31
Vanguard Justice Society v. Hughes, 471 F. Supp.
   670 (D. Md. 1979)   23
Van Hoomissen v. Xerox Corp., 368 F. Supp. 829
   (N.D. Cal. 1973)   19

Wells v. Hutchinson, 25 E.P.D. ¶ 31,689 (E.D. Tex. 1980)	31
Wertz v. Pure Ice Co., 322 F.2d 259 (8th Cir. 1978)	14
Williams v. United States, 341 U.S. 97 (1951)	32
Willis v. Safeway Stores, 17 FEP Cases 102 (N.D. Tex. 1978)	22
Women in City Government, United v. New York, 515 F. Supp. 295 (S.D.N.Y. 1981)	2, 10
Wood v. Strickland, 420 U.S. 308 (1975)	31, 35
Yiamouyiannis v. Chemical Abstracts Service, 521 F.2d 1392 (6th Cir. 1975), *cert. denied*, 439 U.S. 983 (1978)	34
Zises v. Prudential Ins. Co., 25 FEP Cases 557 (D. Mass. 1981)	13

Constitution:

U.S. Constitution:

First Amendment	34
Fifth Amendment	34
Fourteenth Amendment	34

Statutes:

Age Discrimination in Employment Act: 29 U.S.C. § 621 (1980)	1, 12, 13, 14
Civil Rights Act of 1866: 42 U.S.C. § 1981 (1980)	3, 17, 21, 22, 32, 36
Civil Rights Act of 1871: 42 U.S.C. § 1983 (1980) 42 U.S.C. § 1985 (1980)	23, 30, 31
Civil Rights Act of 1964, Title VII: 42 U.S.C. § 2000e, *et seq.* (1980)	1, 7, 10, 12, 14, 18, 19, 32, 33, 36
Equal Pay Act, 29 U.S.C. § 206(d)(1980)	1, 14
Fair Labor Standards Act of 1938, 29 U.S.C. § 201, *et seq.*	14
National Labor Relations Act: 29 U.S.C. § 161, *et seq.* (1980)	1, 3, 7, 12, 14

Rehabilitation Act, 29 U.S.C. §§ 701-794 (1980)	1
28 U.S.C. § 1332 (1980)	17

Executive Order:

Executive Order No. 11246, 3 C.F.R. 169, *codified at* 42 U.S.C. § 2000e (1980)	1

Regulatory Materials:
29 C.F.R. Part 1601.2	8
29 C.F.R. Part 1604.11(c)(1981)	9
EEOC Compliance Manual: Section 2.7	8
EEOC Interpretive Manual: Section 155	8

Legislative Materials:
HOUSE COMM. ON EDUCATION AND LABOR, LABOR-MANAGEMENT RELATIONS ACT, 1947, H. R. Rep. No. 245, 80th Cong., 1st Sess., (1947)	8

Books:
C. Gregory & H. Kalven, *Cases And Materials on Tort Law* (2d ed. 1969)	22
B. Schlei & P. Grossman, *Employment Discrimination Law* (1976)	1, 31
W. Prosser, *Law of Torts* (4th ed. 1971)	16

Miscellaneous:
ABA Model Code of Professional Responsibility: Canon 5 and EC 5-19	28, 29
Willborn, *Insurance, Public Policy And Employment Discrimination*, 66 Minn. L. Rev. 1003 (July 1982)	28
Note, *Limiting The Right To Terminate At Will— —Have The Courts Forgotten the Employer?* 35 Vanderbilt L. Rev. 201 (January 1982)	2

KF 3464 .L48 1982
Levinson, Daniel R.
Personal liability of
 managers and supervisors